# OFFICIAL IMAGES

Smithsonian Institution Press
Washington, D.C.   London

# OFFICIAL IMAGES

## *New Deal Photography*

Pete Daniel
Merry A. Foresta
Maren Stange
Sally Stein

Printed in the United States of America

This book was edited by Caroline Newman and designed by Lisa Buck.

Front Cover: Photograph by Jack Delano, courtesy of the Library of Congress. See figure 21.

Back Cover: Photograph by LeRoy Robbins, courtesy of the photographer. See figure 158.

Additional photo credits: figure 6 courtesy of Oakland Museum; figures 50 and 54 courtesy of *Extension Review Magazine,* Extension Service, USDA; figure 118 courtesy of *Parade* magazine.

Text credits: The Rare Book and Manuscript Library, Columbia University, generously granted permission to quote from the Daniel Longwell papers. Figure 5 text reprinted by permission of Houghton Mifflin.

Library of Congress Cataloging-in-Publication Data

Official images.
Contents:
"The record itself" /
Maren Stange—
Command performances /
Pete Daniel—
Publicity, husbandry, and technocracy /
Maren Stange—[etc.]
1. Photography, Documentary—United States.
2. New Deal, 1933–1939—Pictorial works.
3. United States—Social conditions—1933–1945—Pictorial works.
4. United States—Economic conditions—1933–1945—Pictorial works.
I. Daniel, Pete.
II. Title: New Deal photography.
TR820.5.033 1987 770'.973
87-600050
ISBN 0-87474-349-4 (alk. paper)

British Library Cataloguing-in-Publication data is available.

∞ The paper used in this publication meets the minimum requirements of the American National Standard for Permanence of Paper for Printed Library Materials Z39.48—1984.

# Contents

# A Note on Photograph Captions

Rather than representing modern titles, the captions accompanying the photographs at the end of each essay contain information originally supplied by the photographer—whose name is given whenever known—or in some cases by an editor working in an agency's publicity unit. The order of caption elements has been standardized to place the title and explanatory text first, followed by the location and date, if part of the original documentation. Annotations supplied by the authors are enclosed within brackets. For information on sources and credits, consult the separate listing at the back of the book.

# List of Abbreviations

| | |
|---|---|
| AAA | Agricultural Adjustment Administration |
| CCC | Civilian Conservation Corps |
| FERA | Federal Emergency Relief Administration |
| FSA | Farm Security Administration |
| NYA | National Youth Administration |
| PWAP | Public Works of Art Project |
| RA | Resettlement Administration |
| REA | Rural Electrification Administration |
| USDA | United States Department of Agriculture |
| WPA | Works Progress Administration |
| WPA/FAP★ | WPA Federal Art Project |

★ This is a modern composite abbreviation used to refer to the WPA Federal Art Project (1935–39) which became the Art Program of the Work Projects Administration of the Federal Works Agency (1939–42) and ended as the Graphic Section of the War Services Division (1942–43).

# Preface

This book grew out of the authors' shared interest in mounting an exhibition of little-known documentary photographs at the National Museum of American History. Among government-sponsored images, those captured by the photographers working for the Farm Security Administration (FSA) have long been taken to epitomize thirties photography, yet numerous "official images" from other agencies add significant breadth to the pictorial record of the New Deal. From the beginning a book was planned that would both bring these photographs before a larger audience and place them in a critical historical context.

Written expressly for this volume, the following essays explore in depth the photographic work of five government agencies. Coming from different scholarly backgrounds, the authors pose a variety of questions—ranging from the political to the aesthetic—about the origin and distribution of agency photographs and the impact they may have had in promoting as well as recording aspects of the New Deal experience.

The authors would like to thank the many people who helped make this book possible. Arthur Molella, chairman of the Department of the History of Science and Technology at the National Museum of American History, encouraged this project in numerous ways. The staff at the National Archives were generous with time and suggestions for research. James C. Rush, Jr., reference archivist at the National Archives, guided the authors to the proper records. Aloha South, Richard Crawford, and Charles Roberts aided our search for elusive documents relating to publicity. Barbara Burger, assistant chief for reference in the Still Pictures Branch,

lent her own time and that of her staff, especially Paul White, Deborah Edge, Jim Trimble, Jonathan Hiller, Ouida Brown, and Sharon Culley. Bobbye West and Hugh Talman of the Special Media Preservation Branch produced superior prints from the archive's negatives.

Mary Ison and Majo Felaco at the Prints and Photographs Division of the Library of Congress helped locate images from the FSA file. The staff at the Archives of American Art and researcher Sandra Beller gathered information on the Federal Art Project (FAP). Special thanks go to Arnold Eagle, LeRoy Robbins, and Alexander Alland for supplying firsthand information about their work as FAP photographers, and to Rondal Partridge and Harold Corsini for information on the National Youth Administration. Douglas Helms, historian at the Soil Conservation Service, offered valuable suggestions on sources and photographs relating to the Civilian Conservation Corps. Marjorie Berry, secretary in the Division of Agriculture and Natural Resouces at the National Museum of American History, typed the manuscript and kept track of correspondence. The authors also wish to express special thanks for the support of Diane Hamilton, Nancy Bercaw, Annetta Kapon, Alan Wallach, and Allan Sekula. At the Smithsonian Institution Press, Kathy Kuhtz and Caroline Newman added much-appreciated patience and enthusiasm to impressive editorial skills. The designer, Lisa Buck, created an imaginative interplay of the visual and the textual.

The acquisition of photographs and the research and writing of this book were generously supported by the National Rural Utilities Cooperative Finance Corporation.

# Introduction

Pete Daniel
Sally Stein

No one to date has adequately explained photography's popularity in the midst of the Depression. It was an era of sacrifices, big and little, yet photographs tended to be treated as a necessity. Many felt compelled to take photos and nearly everyone felt compelled to look at them. General statistics on the photographic market did not begin to be collected until after World War II, but analysts of consumer trends seemed to agree that even though the camera bug was an expensive hobby in the Depression, it was a bug reaching epidemic proportions.[1] Maybe the answer is simple. Maybe people feeling deprived of material goods were attracted to those images that most closely resembled the look, surface, and solidity of *things*. Maybe, too, people feeling suddenly insecure about the future were comforted by photography's apparent matter-of-factness, even when the "facts" were often distressing. Most likely, the appeal of photography contained contradictory impulses: to document *and* transform, to gain familiarity *and* distance.

However you explain the popularity of photography in this era, one certain legacy of the Depression is a rich deposit of photographs. Indeed for those born after the thirties, the New Deal era is conceived primarily as a series of images—of Franklin D. Roosevelt, dust storms, bread lines, and migrants moving across the country. Photographs have come to embody some of the anxiety, bitterness, and hope of this epoch. A large number of the decade's best-known photographs were produced by the Farm Security Administration (FSA)—Dorothea Lange's "Migrant Mother," Walker Evans's sharecroppers, and Arthur Rothstein's dust storms. These have

been reproduced so often to illustrate the experience of hard times that now we all tend to equate New Deal photography with the emblematic imagery of the FSA. While recent studies of FSA documentary work have gone beyond the classic "cookie cutters" or stereotypes, discussion of government uses of photography in the 1930s has remained limited to a single agency within a single federal department.

Fifty years ago, however, the FSA had no monopoly on New Deal photography. In 1936, Time Inc. conducted a survey of available sources of picture material as part of the groundwork of putting together *Life* magazine, that preeminent vehicle for thirties photography. On returning from an out-of-town reconnaissance mission, a staff picture researcher announced to her New York colleagues that Washington was the center of the photographic field. In the nation's capital could be found foreign photo collections maintained by embassies and every major archive of the federal government. Though she briefly described the photographic contents of a few choice agencies, her report emphasized that practically *all* government departments kept complete photographic records of their activities. According to this researcher, most were "exceptionally fine." To dispel any lingering doubts about the quality of government-issue pictures, she singled out the work of the Soil Conservation Service which she judged to be "of Margaret Bourke-White quality."[2] This was high praise indeed at the magazine offices where Margaret Bourke-White was the top-ranking staff photographer.

The FSA was mentioned by its original name, the

Resettlement Administration (RA), but it figured in this memo as just one of many government agencies with sizable photographic collections, including the Rural Electrification Administration, the United States Department of Agriculture (USDA), the Department of the Interior, and the especially noteworthy Soil Conservation Service. This researcher's findings were consistent with other primary sources from the 1930s. One of the earliest Depression-era picture anthologies, *The Roosevelt Year: A Photographic Record* (1934), made extensive use of contemporary government pictures before the RA/FSA photography unit had been established. The book's editor, Pare Lorentz—who subsequently worked with the FSA offices producing some of the most celebrated documentary films of the era—drew upon New Deal collections not even covered in the Time Inc. survey, namely, the Tennessee Valley Authority, the Civil Works Administration, and the Public Works Administration. A similar photographic anthology published a year later, *Eyes on the World,* overlooked the RA/FSA collection but made extensive use of photographs from the USDA. Yet another oversize photo anthology, published in 1938, credited for source material the RA, the Federal Emergency Relief Administration, the Tennessee Valley Authority, and the National Research Project of the Works Progress Administration.[3]

Any recitation of the government's tongue-twisting names for relief agencies suggests that the New Deal was more adept with images than words. Comparing the Progressive era of the turn of the century with the New Deal two decades later, historian Warren Susman marked the end of a culture centered on the book. This "shift to a culture of sight and sound"[4] was well underway when Franklin Roosevelt first took office in 1933. Early in the 1920s radio gained popularity, initially as a mechanical fad but by the end of the decade as a dependable form of entertainment and information. In 1927 moviegoers welcomed talkies; sound recording technology was crucial for the new Hollywood feature film and also for the newsreel report that regularly accompanied it in movie houses. No less than the popularization of radio and movies, the launching of *Life* and *Look* magazines in the mid-thirties transformed the nation's reading habits. Millions of readers who previously had studied photographs reproduced as grainy newspaper illustrations became avid consumers of weekly doses of high-resolution, glossy photographs that now were the centerpiece of news stories.

The Roosevelt administration was eager to exploit these media innovations. With his "Fireside Chats," the president personally set a standard for radio showmanship. But just as Congress through much of the thirties tried to resist the expansion of executive power, it also fought hard to control the amount and character of government publicity. Despite the fact that corporate advertising was visibly transforming American society at the turn of the century, Congress as early as 1913 began legislating against similar activity by the federal government.[5] The conservative prejudice against government publicity persisted and even grew deeper in the thirties. Indeed throughout the Depression Congress repeatedly voiced two arguments against any innovations in government publicity techniques. Not only did skillful publicity usually amount to an added budgetary expense; if effective it could also be expected to rally public support for "priming the pump"—the New Deal's general fiscal policy of stimulating the economy by creating massive relief programs. Perhaps herein lies the motive for the characteristic "documentary" style of New Deal publicity—a style that *looked* candid, intimate yet non-intrusive, even as it promoted the value of forceful, bureaucratic government intervention to shore up a stagnant economy.

In response to frequent charges of propaganda, defenders of New Deal publicity countered that government relief measures in a time of crisis were useless if kept a secret from the public. Furthermore, liberal students of public administration—and they were a growing breed in this era—often pointed out the discrepancy between the amount of advertising deployed by the private and public sector, thus assuaging fears that government propaganda would lead directly to a totalitarian regime. One such student, James L. McCamy, produced a doctoral dissertation that frankly applauded those government offices experimenting aggressively with promotional uses of photography, pictographs, radio, and the like. McCamy's study also demonstrated a direct correlation between the use of modern media strategies and the new crop of federal agencies lacking established constituencies. His prime example was the FSA, an agency staffed by young professionals, unhampered by traditional concepts of government and modes of communication, and responsible for producing a distinctive style of photography that emphasized human consequences of the agricultural crisis rather than clinical, topographic details.[6]

But experiments with new media techniques were not confined to the ad hoc New Deal offices. By 1937 the venerable USDA felt obliged to coordinate the activities of its various branches and to set priorities for films, radio, talks, photographs, and exhibits.[7] Predictably, the expanding publicity work of the USDA was subjected to close scrutiny. In 1938 Congressman J. Parnell Thomas requested of Secretary of Agriculture Henry A. Wallace the names, salaries, types of activities, and titles of employees engaged in publicity, as well as the publications issued by the department. Mindful of the legal restrictions on government publicity, Wallace downplayed the significance of the department's 2,300 press releases, insisting they only presented "the results of research in a manner that will make these results of greatest value to the public" or reported on "the regularity, service, and conservation programs of the Department." The letter containing this disavowal, however, ran twenty-nine pages in order to supply a complete accounting of specialists, media projects, and publications financed by the department.[8]

Obviously, the use of photographs was just one feature of the New Deal's overall public relations effort, for the government availed itself of every popular medium to fashion sophisticated justifications for its policies. The National Archives—itself a period monument to the New Deal's reverence for government documents—contains extensive evidence of radio broadcasts, exhibits, filmstrips, and films. Official images were only part of the New Deal's self-styled record, but the questions they provoke are largely applicable to other aspects of government publicity in the Great Depression.

This book grew out of a shared interest in the vast, unexplored accumulation of New Deal photography. Since FSA imagery is exceptionally well-known today, we suspected that it was also exceptional at the time. But without any basis for comparison we had no idea how exceptional, or in what ways. One reason why FSA pictures have long been considered incomparable is their physical accessibility: housed in the Prints and Photographs Division of the Library of Congress, the FSA

collection of approximately seventy-five thousand prints is organized to facilitate use by the general public whereas the rest of New Deal agency photographs are maintained in closed stacks in the National Archives. Some pictures have been more visible than others. These institutional patterns of "open" and "closed" files may help explain the limited scope of current discussions of government documentary photography. Yet a contextual understanding of thirties documentary practice is impossible without a broader sampling from the period.

Thus we compiled representative imagery from five different sources in the New Deal: the United States Department of Agriculture (USDA), the Works Progress Administration (WPA), the National Youth Administration (NYA), the Civilian Conservation Corps (CCC), as well as the Farm Security Administration (FSA). These five agencies produced an enormous range as well as quantity of New Deal photography. The constituency and policy objectives differed with each agency, and especially in the thirties photographers working for the government had enormously varied backgrounds. Older agencies tended to rely upon photographers who had long been part of the civil service and whose concepts and methods of producing government publicity were developed in an older economic and photographic era. In addition to these veterans, New Deal photographers ranged from sheer novices and gifted amateurs to beleaguered professionals who turned to the government for employment (indeed, the pioneer American social documentary photographer Lewis Hine was reduced in this period to begging various federal agencies for assignments after decades of working independently).[9] A number of painters and printmakers also became government photographers during the Depression; some made this change primarily for lack of other work but others actively sought a more modern, less rarefied medium with which to represent the conditions of social crisis. Recent technological innovations—faster films, miniature cameras, portable synchronized flashlights—permitted rank amateurs as well as artists to quickly assume the role of photographer. This role was not necessarily a full-time pursuit. Regional administrators often supplied visual documentation of local projects, and in a few agencies—especially youth agencies—ordinary clients sometimes had the opportunity to document the programs.

Given this motley crew, it is not surprising that the resulting collections of pictures would vary wildly in terms of technical proficiency, artistic sensibility, political acumen, and personal and social commitment. In order to capture some of this diversity, we have purposefully sought to sustain rather than gloss over the variations and inconsistencies in style and perspective. From the photographic record of each agency, we have selected hackneyed work as well as visually dynamic and novel imagery. Yet this refusal to privilege the "greatest hits" is more than an attempt to register the surprising range of official imagery. Often the conventional, formulaic pictures provide telling clues to both visual style and social emphasis in the thirties.

In researching agency files, we not only considered *our* principles of selection, but paid careful attention to evidence of prior editing and selection in the original construction of these archives. Just as important as the taking of photographs was what happened to them after they were made. Before being used by an agency, photographs went through a filtering process. The job of publicity managers was to legitimate bureaucratic authority; not unreasonably, they often excluded those views that could weaken the institutional validity of their particular agency. Photographers usually acted on agency instructions, hunting for assigned subjects. Once photographers submitted work to a central office, editors selected those pictures suitable for their needs, often attempting to verify with *particular* images *general* New Deal stereotypes. In some cases, editors altered or omitted captions or cropped photographs to exclude undesirable information. Usually these changes were minor, justifiable forms of editorial discretion, but occasionally cropping and captioning served clear political ends. In retrospect, then, the visual publicity efforts of these agencies are important both for what photographers and bureaucrats explicitly intended and for the tacit political statements they made, whether revealed in unacknowledged details or in details deliberately suppressed. We would be missing the point if we studied these images only as they pertained to the formation of a documentary style of representation. Government photography was intended to influence public policy and opinion; indeed, that was its reason for being. The larger the federal government grew, the more it depended upon popular graphic forms to convince people that government intervention was beneficial and proper.

Maybe it's best to confess failures at the outset. When the authors of this project first convened to discuss strategy and objectives, we envisioned a survey of photographs from the full panoply of New Deal agencies. On the other hand, we rejected outright the formalist model of a superficial collection of New Deal pictures divorced from specific institutional contexts. After only a short time spent in the archives reviewing textual records as well as files of still pictures, we realized the folly of our ambition. Without enlisting an army of fellow researchers (and finding the funds to support them), we would need to sacrifice either breadth or depth. So we narrowed down to a study of five agencies, deliberately including the FSA as a shared point of reference (though Maren Stange's essay on this agency represents a significant revisionist analysis of this familiar photographic field). What results is a beginning rather than an end, suggesting possibilities for reevaluation rather than definitive conclusions. Now we can begin to analyze more precisely how FSA photography departed from established government photographic conventions. And to the extent that FSA photography established new standards for government publicity, we also can consider the effect—sometimes inspiring, sometimes restrictive or inappropriate—of these standards on other agencies. With alternative models at hand, we are better able to weigh the relative significance of certain types of iconography, photographic style, editorial handling, and channels of distribution—all elements contributing to the production and reception of photographic publicity.

We hoped that with sufficient research we could see the forest rather than the largest and arguably most stunning tree. For now we are content with a somewhat broader though still limited perspective. If this set of essays provokes new research on publicity in government sources—the archives of the Tennessee Valley Authority, Army Corps of Engineers, Soil Conservation Service, and Social Security Act seemed to us especially rich prospects for further work—we may yet grasp the vast enterprise of social documentation at the center of the New Deal.

# Notes

1. Information on industrywide trends in the photographic market became regularly available in 1952 with the annual publication of Augustus Wolfman's *Report on the Photographic Industry*. Previously Eastman Kodak sought to guard its market research, probably to avoid stimulating competitive enterprises, so that the only figures Kodak made available in this period were the general earnings report required by law. Except for three years, Kodak could boast a healthy rate of profit throughout the thirties (see graph of new profits since 1915 in Eastman Kodak's Annual Report of 1938, p. 24). For independent analysis of expansion of the photographic market of the 1930s, see Roland S. Vaile, *Research Memorandum on Social Aspects of Consumption in the Depression* (New York, 1937), 25–26, and a *Fortune* article, "The U.S. Minicam Boom," reporting (with statistics provided by German manufacturers) on camera buying trends at the high end of the market, *Fortune* 14:4 (October 1936), 124–29, and 160–70. For a literary account of specifically working class interest in photography at this time, see Thomas Bell's proletarian novel, *Out of this Furnace* (Boston, 1941), chapter 14, 362–77.

2. Patricia West, "Washington Report," in the archive of *Life* editor, Daniel Longwell, "Picture Bureau" file, Box 27, Daniel Longwell papers, Rare Book and Manuscript Library, Columbia University. Though West was operating under the impression that she was researching possibilities for a picture agency, the agency project was actually a cover for preparatory work on *Life*, according to Robert T. Elson's account, *Time Inc.* (New York, 1968), 274.

3. Pare Lorentz, ed., *The Roosevelt Year* (New York, 1934), iv; M. Lincoln Schuster, ed., *Eyes on the World* (New York, 1935), 292–93; S. A. Spencer, *The Greatest Show on Earth* (Garden City, N.Y., 1938), 188–89.

4. Warren I. Susman, *Culture as History* (New York, 1984), 161.

5. James L. McCamy, *Government Publicity* (Chicago, 1939), 5–12.

6. McCamy cites a number of contemporaneous unpublished dissertations in the preface to the 1939 publication of his doctoral study, p. viii; for persuasive evidence demonstrating that newer agencies as a rule were most willing to experiment with new forms of communication, see pp. 221–45.

7. For the development of coordinated publicity in the USDA, see Lester A. Schlup to J. R. Fleming, May 17, 1937; Fleming to Schlup, May 29, 1937; Keith Himebaught, memo to Milton S. Eisenhower, October 9, 1939; G. A. Barnes, memo to Morse Salisbury, January 31, 1940; Salisbury, memo to Leon O. Wolcott, January 27, 1940; Salisbury, memo to Paul H. Appleby, May 10, 1940, and attached report, "Report of Informal Committee on Visual Information," Office of Information, General Correspondence, 1913–44; Joseph W. Hiscox to Reuben Brigham, March 16, 1939; Brigham to Appleby, March 23, 1939, General Correspondence, Extension Work, Records of the Secretary of Agriculture, Record Group 16, National Archives (hereafter cited SOA, RG 16, NA).

8. Henry A. Wallace to J. Parnell Thomas, June 2, 1938, General Correspondence, Publicity, SOA, RG 16, NA.

9. Walter Rosenblum recalls Hine's desperate personal situation in the thirties in his foreword to *America and Lewis Hine* (Millerton, N.Y., 1977), 9–11.

# "The Record Itself":

*Farm Security Administration Photography and the Transformation of Rural Life*

## Maren Stange

Conceived to serve more functions than the programs of other New Deal agencies, the massive Farm Security Administration (FSA) photography project generated some 270,000 images of rural, urban, and industrial America between 1935 and 1943. Redefining the idea of government publicity in a manner at once subtle and grand, the project offered its dozen-odd photographers "enormous possibilities," as Walker Evans wrote in 1935. Excited by his appointment to the FSA, Evans did not anticipate making "photographic statements for the government or do[ing] photographic chores" because, as seemed evident to him, "the value and, if you like, even the propaganda value for the government lies in the record itself which in the long run will prove an intelligent and farsighted thing to have done."[1] Virtually from the start, the FSA aimed at more than producing file photographs for Washington bureaus or generating local publicity and good will for government relief measures. By hiring photographers such as Evans, Ben Shahn, and Dorothea Lange, whose training, abilities, and ambitions far exceeded those of most other agency photographers, the FSA set the high standards that have made it justly famous (figs. 1–4). In addition, project director Roy Stryker early established an extensive network among journalists, editors, and publishers that ensured FSA photographs were widely seen.

Supported by a staff that included photographer and designer Edwin Rosskam—hired solely to design exhibits and promote the use of agency photographs—Stryker saw to it that, by 1938, FSA photographs had appeared in *Time, Fortune, Today, Look,* and *Life* (as well

as *Junior Scholastic* and the Lubbock, Texas, *Morning Avalanche*). They were exhibited at the Museum of Modern Art and the Democratic National Convention of 1936. By 1940, they had been published in nearly a dozen books, including Walker Evans's *American Photographs,* Archibald MacLeish's *Land of the Free,* Herman Nixon's *Forty Acres and Steel Mules,* and Dorothea Lange and Paul Taylor's *An American Exodus: A Record of Human Erosion* (figs. 5 and 6).[2] Some images, such as Lange's "Migrant Mother," Arthur Rothstein's "Dust Bowl," or Russell Lee's "Hands," became almost instant icons because of their appealing, even pleasurable, humanitarian rhetoric (fig. 7). Articulating "the philosophy of the documentary approach," as project director Roy Stryker called it, they were readily presented and received as visual analogues of the social concern that motivated the novels of John Steinbeck, the documentary dramas of the Federal Theatre Project, the songs of Woody Guthrie, or the murals and graphics of the federal arts projects. Indeed, as writer James Agee pointed out in the thirties, the camera was "the central instrument of our time," and the FSA's graphically appealing, mass-reproducible images made a poignant contribution to the emerging mass culture formed by radio, photojournalism, and movies.[3]

The FSA begin in 1935 as the Resettlement Administration (RA), an independent coordinating agency that inherited rural relief activities and land-use administration from the Department of the Interior, the Federal Emergency Relief Administration, and the Agricultural Adjustment Administration. Many of the projects we now associate with the FSA—cooperative rural resettlement communities, rehabilitation loans and grants for small farmers, farm debt adjustment, migrant camps, and erosion and flood control—had already been initiated by these government agencies. Rexford Tugwell, the Roosevelt Brains Truster who became the first (and only) administrator of the RA, coordinated the various programs under the theory that a reorganization and reform of agriculture along industrial lines could be accomplished by the "rehabilitation of poor people and poor land together in one federal agency."[4] The RA was organized into four divisions: national land-use planning; rural rehabilitation, which administered loans and grants to individuals and groups of farmers; and rural resettlement and suburban resettlement, two experimental programs that developed planned communities, among them the famous Greenbelt towns. In 1937, the RA lost its independent status; the agency was retitled FSA and subsumed under the Department of Agriculture. Although at this point the agency concentrated on providing loans, subsistence funds, and other "immediate or emergency" relief, it never entirely abandoned the experimental efforts at long-term planning Tugwell had established.[5] The photography project, officially titled the Historical Section–Photographic, was set up as part of an Information Division responsible for all publicity pertaining to the RA and later the FSA; it was intended to publicize not only the long-standing rural distress that had necessitated such unprecedented federal intervention, but also the ameliorative effects and the unique long-range goals of agency programs.

In many ways, the broad scope of the FSA culminated a social vision initiated by progressive reformers early in the century. These thinkers saw the major goal of American reform as an effort to adjust all social classes to the new "economy of abundance" that had been achieved through mass production. Privileging the work of planners, social scientists, and social workers, reformers expected these professionals to develop and promote "new ideals of human behavior appropriate to an economy of abundance"; they relied heavily on social institutions and the mass media to begin a "program of constructive mass education in the ways of better living."[6]

These "technicians of reform" were ambivalent at best toward workers' or farmers' efforts to help themselves through class-conscious organizations of their own.[7] Thus despite the inevitable deskilling, speedup, and loss of work place control entailed by scientific management, Rexford Tugwell supported this increasingly technocratic industrial system, along with company unions, because it promoted a "friendly cooperation with workers" appropriate to the new age of abundance and corporate economic organization. Traditional industrial unionism, he maintained, only continued "the suspicious driving of the system inherited from entrepreneurial industrial organization." His writings, like those of other progressives, proposed in effect that progress and modernity required a reorientation and "modernization" of working class values. In such a view, real reform could only be accomplished if there were a harmony between workers and managers in which workers' values came to resemble and reinforce, rather than to oppose, the values and ideology of the technocratic elite that had emerged to manage American industry after World War I.[8]

Tugwell was Roy Stryker's mentor and helped introduce him to such a progressive worldview in the 1920s, when Stryker was Tugwell's student and teaching assistant at Columbia and a part-time settlement house worker. As picture editor for Tugwell's economics text, *American Economic Life and the Means of Its Improvement,* Stryker became expert at using photography to dramatize Tugwell's social ideology (see fig. 8). Though Stryker was no theorist, his conception of the FSA photography project was clearly influenced by a progressive vision that welcomed modernization and technocratic efficiency as a way to "uplift" standards of rural and urban American life.[9]

As history makes evident, the FSA project, despite its stated concern to preserve the "decency" and "dignity" of rural people, was actually recording the irreversible exodus of farmers from the land and their consequent status as a newly dislocated proletariat. In their documentary book, *An American Exodus,* Dorothea Lange and Paul Taylor showed there was no going back, for mechanization had penetrated farming methods themselves and changed them forever. Farm foreclosures and the forced migration of small farmers in the 1930s resulted not only from drought and soil erosion, but also from the introduction of mechanized methods that required less labor and encouraged large-scale operations. As Paul Taylor described a typical situation, "only 30 families remain to work at day labor where 160 share-cropper families lived on the land. Twenty-two tractors and 13 four-row cultivators have replaced 130 families."[10] And despite the FSA's proclamation of "greater obligation to poorer farm families" and "successful rehabilitation through better farm and home practices," government policies actually encouraged the trend. "Landlords clash with their tenants over the crop reduction check, not openly or in organized fashion," Paul Taylor wrote; "but the landlords force tenants off the place, they use the government checks and their own livestock as payments on tractors, so more and more tenants 'can't get a farm.' "[11] Figure 9, recording such a clash, shows a roadside demonstration by Missouri sharecroppers evicted because of acreage reduction policies; rather than departing peacefully, they have camped on the roads until removed by state troopers.

In the far-reaching conclusions of their book, Lange and Taylor, observing that mechanization "should not, and probably cannot be halted," urged government policies that would not deny "participation in the advantages of a machine-produced standard of living to . . . farmers for subsistence." They argued that "the real opportunity for large-scale absorption of the displaced must lie in the direction of industrial expansion, not in crowding [farmers] back onto the land where already they are surplus."[12] Among the most interesting photographs in the FSA file are those showing precisely this painful and gradual process of absorption (figs. 10–34). As the often extensive supporting documentation makes clear, photographers sought out the details of farmers' accommodations to the exigencies of mechanization and industrialism; in the process they photographed many kinds of people, not all of them dignified or decent, and they often eschewed, in favor of more complex statements, the appealing graphic rhetoric that made successes of the great icons. These images poignantly document the massive and irreversible breakdown of traditional rural life, and they also portray an often obscured reality: the similarity between rural and working class social actualities that prevailed in the 1930s because farm dwellers, impoverished by long-standing agricultural depression, had sought work in local textile factories, saw mills, and food-processing plants.

Dorothea Lange's photographs of the "factories in the fields" of the Imperial Valley and of dreary highways and migrant camps where "Okies" vied for jobs with Japanese, Filipino, black, and Mexican workers must be counted among the classic records of such dislocation and exploitation (figs. 27–34). They are complemented by photographs from other parts of the United States that show how former farmers, beset by forces beyond their control, were funneled into the hearts of cities or scattered in outlying shantytowns, lured to the hot and noisy rooms of textile mills, to oil field camps, construction sites, and, eventually, defense boomtowns (figs. 10–19). In some images, those who would seem to be most enmeshed in industrial life retain the most identifiably rural appearance: the wives of striking oil field workers look as if they are preparing a harvest meal (fig. 16); the man who has left the farm for construction work retains his ruddy cheeks and farming clothes (fig. 18), as does the young wife at the table of union literature supplied by the United Cannery, Agricultural, Packing and Allied Workers of America (UCAPAWA) (fig. 20). In some images the pieced quilt, now doing duty in tents, trailers, and shacks, is a nostalgic remainder of displacement (figs. 17, 27). In others, the caption proffers an unexpected detail that makes a crucial statement: despite their quintessentially urban appearance, the men at the sewing machines at Levine and Levine's ladies' coat factory in Colchester live and work on nearby farms (fig. 10); in a 1940 photograph, the Andrews family pose around the kitchen table in their farmhouse without father or husband, because he is away doing day labor in construction for the Army (fig. 21).

As Lange had done in California, other photographers traced the steps beyond the harvest that transformed agricultural produce into commodities to be consumed. Since the production and distribution of produce had long entailed a series of mechanized processes, their documentation led photographers to olive oil factories, pecan shelling sheds, stockyards, cotton gins, and turpentine stills (fig. 22). Yet despite photographers' visits to such work places, or to homes and social gatherings, proportionately few images in the file show workers' organized responses to the generally wretched conditions of agricultural production. It is as if the fervor of a Steinbeck meeting speaker or the collectivity of striking King Farm workers, while admirable in themselves, were too intense in content, too demanding of social explanation, to serve successfully the ever increasing publicity function of the file (figs. 25, 26).

Thus, though many situations were heavily documented and the photographers were plainly engaged by the material, the details of exploitation and resistance that might dramatize the emergence of a new consciousness among former farmers appear only piecemeal and by chance: Library of Congress supplementary reference file material tells us, for instance, that the protested wage cut at the King Farm was from twenty-five to twenty cents an hour for men and from twenty to seventeen cents for women; in San Antonio, unionized Mexican pecan workers enlisted the National Labor Relations Board in their fight against the imposition of a ninety-day "learner's" period with wages of 15 cents an hour (fig. 22). The former Oklahoma farmer whom Lange photographed in Kern County, California (fig. 29), had been a leader in the cotton strike of 1938 and drove the first car of a squadron that attempted to penetrate and picket the large fields of corporate farms by automobile caravan. His union, the UCAPAWA, is the same one that called the meeting in Oklahoma (fig. 20); in a Mexican town outside of Shafter, California, as another Lange photograph shows us, a crowd of strikers (whose strike eventually failed) listens to a UCAPAWA representative (fig. 28).[13]

Such suggestive images sketch out, if they do not fully represent, a working class, a collectivity, and they imply its antithesis, the social atomization even then being imposed by mass culture and technocracy. The FSA was "a relentlessly ambitious fact-finding machine which was, at the same time, carefully self-censoring," as art historian Terence Smith describes it; what the agency omitted, as much as what it included, reveals the terms on which such a government-sponsored project might exist in a time of great and painful change. Yet in tracing, however partially, the consciousness of farmers throughout what Smith calls "the social networks in which agricultural production is enmeshed," photographers engaged material that pushed against the limitations set by the project's ideological presumptions.[14] The photographic representation of complex social situations subverted official ideology. Neither affirming traits of character displayed in farmers' struggles with drought, dust, and sharecrop tenancy, nor celebrating the government's "rehabilitative" rural projects, these images instead set forth the details of the processes by which displaced farmers coped, in however debilitated a fashion, with corporate exploitation, with modernization, and with whatever scraps of "abundance" were available to them. In its published material, the FSA reaffirmed established documentary conventions that focused on individual victims and/or heroes, and it used them to enhance and humanize its programmatic vision. But the larger photographic record held in the Library of Congress files gains meaning and power from images, like those we have seen, that mark out the territory of real and vast social change. Had the FSA fully explored that territory, its photography might have depicted not only collectivity, but also, and critically, the atomization, so powerfully imposed by mass culture, with which collectivity contended.

As war approached, the need for a yet more ideological and abstracted industrial image became more pressing and constraining. In a famous memo, Stryker called in 1942 for photographs of "people with a little spirit," particularly "young men and women who work in our factories, [and] the young men who build our bridges, roads, dams and large factories." As the Historical Section–Photographic was transferred to the Office of War Information, and the FSA itself fought to survive in the face of Congressional attacks, the possibilities for complex representation grew slimmer. Stryker wanted "pictures of men, women and children who appear as if they really believed in the U.S.," and he urged photographers to concentrate on "shipyards, steel mills, aircraft plants, oil refineries, and always the happy American worker." Their images came to look, according to photographer John Vachon, discouragingly "like those from the Soviet Union" (see fig. 35).[15]

Finding that his position had changed from "editorial director to . . . administrative operator," and that the section had become—as he wrote to Dorothea Lange—"a service organization . . . maintaining the files, running the laboratory, and hunting pictures from other Government Agencies," Stryker resigned from the FSA in 1943 and went to work in corporate public relations for the Standard Oil Company of New Jersey. The new job, Stryker claimed, would help him "find out how the other half of America lives." It seems, on the ideological and representational evidence of his FSA work, that that corporate and technocratic half was one Stryker already knew a lot about.[16]

# Notes

1. Walker Evans, *Walker Evans at Work* (New York, 1982), 112.

2. Walker Evans, *American Photographs* (New York, 1962; originally published 1938); Herman C. Nixon, *Forty Acres and Steel Mules* (Chapel Hill, 1938). Newspaper and magazine titles for 1937 and 1938 are from monthly and biweekly reports from the Historical Section–Photographic to James Fischer, Director of Information, and are located in Historical Section Textual Records, Box 4, Farm Security Administration, Prints and Photographs Division, Library of Congress (hereafter cited as FSA, PPD, LC). See also F. Jack Hurley, *Portrait of a Decade: Roy Stryker and the Development of Documentary Photography in the Thirties* (Baton Rouge, 1974), chapter 6; Karin Becker Ohrn, *Dorothea Lange and the Documentary Tradition* (Baton Rouge, 1980), 109; interview with Ben Shahn by Richard Doud, April 14, 1964, Archives of American Art, Smithsonian Institution, Washington, D.C. (also in New York, Boston, Detroit and Los Angeles; hereafter cited as AAA).

3. Stryker quoted in William Stott, *Documentary Expression and Thirties America* (New York, 1973), ix; James Agee and Walker Evans, *Let Us Now Praise Famous Men* (Boston, 1941), 11.

4. Sidney Baldwin, *Poverty and Politics: The Rise and Decline of the Farm Security Administration* (Chapel Hill, 1968), 88; Tugwell quoted in Bernard Sternsher, *Rexford Tugwell and the New Deal* (New Brunswick, 1964), 265.

5. See Baldwin, *Poverty and Politics,* for a history of the agency; for Tugwell's policies, see Resettlement Administration, *First Annual Report of the Resettlement Administration* (Washington: U.S. Government Printing Office, 1936) and Rexford G. Tugwell, "The Place of Government in a National Land Program" *Journal of Farm Economics* 16, (January 1934), 55–69.

6. Simon N. Patten, *The New Basis of Civilization* (New York, 1907), 10, quoted in Daniel M. Fox, *The Discovery of Abundance* (Ithaca, 1967), 97–98, 100.

7. On progressive reformers, see Samuel Haber, *Efficiency and Uplift: Scientific Management in the Progressive Era, 1890–1920* (Chicago, 1964); Roy Lubove, *The Progressives and the Slums: Tenement House Reform in New York City 1890–1917* (Pittsburgh, 1962); and Robert H. Wiebe, *The Search for Order, 1877–1920* (New York, 1967).

8. Rexford Tugwell, *Industry's Coming of Age* (New York,

1927), 32. For a more detailed discussion of Tugwell's ideas and of the influence of Tugwell's mentor, the economist Simon Patten, see my forthcoming *"Symbols of Ideal Life": Social Documentary Photography in America, 1890–1950* (New York, 1988), chapter 3. In " 'Symbols of Ideal Life': Technology, Mass Media, and the FSA Photography Project," *Prospects* 11 (1986), 81–105, I discuss details of the project more fully than is possible here.

9. Rexford Guy Tugwell, Thomas Munro, and Roy E. Stryker, *American Economic Life and the Means of Its Improvement* (New York: 2nd ed., 1924; 3rd ed., 1930). For information on Stryker's collaboration on the textbook, see interview with Roy Stryker by Richard Doud, December 23, 1965, 10–11, AAA; and Hurley, *Portrait of a Decade,* 15–16.

10. Dorothea Lange and Paul Schuster Taylor, *An American Exodus: A Record of Human Erosion* (New York, 1939), 25.

11. United States Department of Agriculture, *Toward Farm Security: The Problem of Rural Poverty and the Work of the Farm Security Administration, Prepared under the Direction of the FSA Personnel Training Committee, for FSA Employees, by Joseph Gaer* (Washington, 1941), 66–67; Paul Taylor to Thomas C. Blaisdell, Jr., June 3, 1937, Series I, Roy Stryker Collection, Photographic Archives, University of Louisville (hereafter cited as UL).

12. Lange and Taylor, *An American Exodus,* 153–54.

13. For information on the King Farm strike, see Lot 1351; for information on the Pecan Shellers' case, see Lot 593, Supplementary Reference File, FSA, PPD, LC.

14. Terence Edwin Smith, "Making the Modern: The Visual Imagery of Modernity, U.S.A., 1908–1939" (Ph.D. diss., University of Sydney, Australia, 1985), 342–43.

15. Roy Emerson Stryker and Nancy Wood, *In This Proud Land: America 1935–1943, As Seen in the FSA Photographs* (Boston, 1973), 188; John Vachon, "Tribute to a Man, an Era, an Art," *Harper's Magazine* (September 1973), 99, quoted in Steven W. Plattner, "How the Other Half Lived: The Standard Oil Company (New Jersey) Photographic Project, 1943–1950" (M.A. thesis, George Washington University, 1981), 30.

16. Roy Stryker, "Official Notice of Resignation," September 14, 1943; Stryker to Dorothea Lange, September 16, 1943; Stryker to John Gaus, September 16, 1943, Stryker Collection, UL, all quoted in Plattner, "How the Other Half Lived," 34–35.

1

*Ben Shahn*

Coal miner's child. Omar,
West Virginia. October 1935.

2

*Walker Evans*

Main Street. Macon, Georgia.
March 1936.

3

*Ben Shahn*

Striking miners. Scott's Run,
West Virginia. October 1935.

4

*Dorothea Lange*

Plantation owner. Near Clarksdale, Mississippi. June 1936.

We told ourselves we were free because we were free.

We were free because we were that kind.

We were Americans.

All you needed for freedom was being American.
All you needed for freedom was grit in your craw
And the gall to get out on a limb and crow before sunup.

Those that hadn't it hadn't it.

"Have the elder races halted?

Do they droop and end their lessons wearied over there beyond the seas?

We take up the task eternal and the burden and the lesson —

Pioneers O Pioneers."

We told ourselves we were free because we said so.

We were free because of the Battle of Bunker Hill
And the constitution adopted at Philadelphia

*5*

[From Archibald MacLeish, *Land of the Free* (New York, 1977 reprint edition), 7. Text copyright 1938 by Archibald MacLeish. Copyright © renewed 1966 by Archibald MacLeish. Reprinted by permission of Houghton Mifflin Company.]

*6*

[From Dorothea Lange and Paul Schuster Taylor, *An American Exodus: A Record of Human Erosion* (New York, 1939), 100–1. The FSA files at the Library of Congress hold a variant of this image, titled, "Wife of Migratory Laborer with three children." Childress (vicinity), Texas. June 1938.]

7

*Arthur Rothstein*

Dust storm. Cimmaron
County, Oklahoma. 1936.

[From Rexford Tugwell, Thomas Munro, and Roy E. Stryker, *American Economic Life and the Means of Its Improvement,* 3rd edition (New York, 1930), 650.]

Workers in the steel industry: (1) Italian; (2) Irish; (3) German; (4) Lithuanian; (5) Polish; (6) Serbian; (7) Russian; (8) Slovak; (9) English; (10) American. (11) Interior of a steel mill. The difficulty of organizing large groups of men for collective bargaining is apparent when the different nationalities involved are considered. (Photos by Hine. Drawing by Vernon Howe Bailey. Courtesy Interstate Steel Company.)

*Arthur Rothstein*

Evicted sharecroppers along
Highway #60. New Madrid
County, Missouri. January
1939.

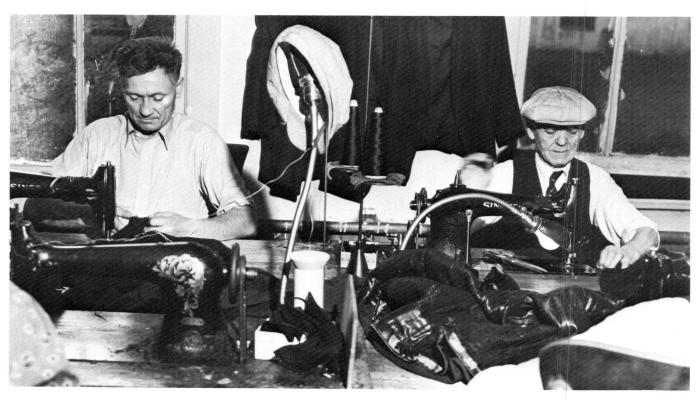

10

*Jack Delano*

Workers in a small ladies'
coat factory, Levine and Levine Ladies' Coats. Most of the
workers live on farms nearby.
Colchester, Connecticut.

*11*

*Russell Lee*

Men sitting on a park bench.
Chicago, Illinois. April 1941.

12

*Russell Lee*

Children. Southside of Chicago, Illinois. April 1941.

*Edwin Rosskam*

Children in front of "kitchen-
ette" apartment. Black Belt,
Chicago, Illinois. April 1941.

*John Vachon*

Foraging for food at the city
dump. Produce houses dump
apples, grapefruit, oranges,
etc. which are not quite bad.
Dubuque, Iowa. April 1940.

15

*Russell Lee*

Home and family of oil field
roustabout. During periods of
unemployment, the woman
takes in washing and ironing.
Oklahoma City, Oklahoma.
August 1939.

*Russell Lee*

Wives of striking members of
Oil Workers Union preparing
lunch for picketers. Seminole,
Oklahoma. August 1939.

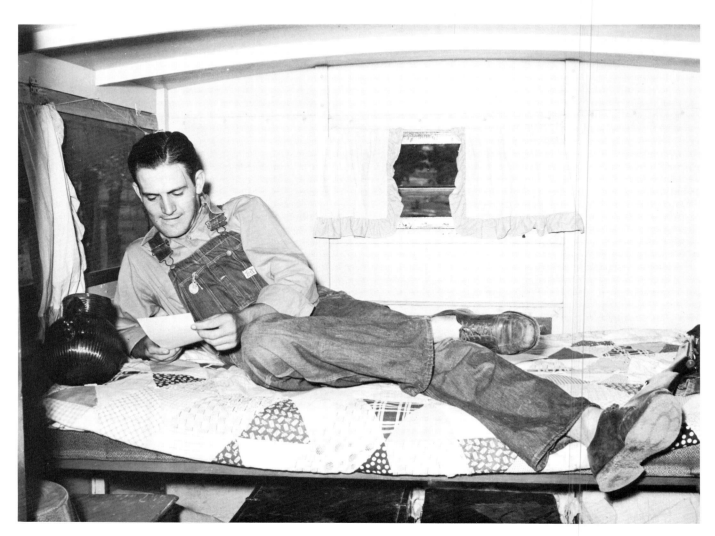

17 _____

*Russell Lee*

Oil field worker in his trailer home reading a letter. Seminole, Oklahoma. August 1939.

18

*John Vachon*

Farm couple from neighboring county who left the farm and followed the boom. Newton County, Missouri. February 1942.

19

*Russell Lee*

Exterior of house of work-
man's family. Corpus Christi,
Texas. December 1940.

20

*Russell Lee*

Mother and children at agri‑
cultural workers' union
meeting. Taber, Oklahoma.
February 1940.

21

*Jack Delano*

The family of Peter V. Andrews, Portuguese. They run
a small 7-acre vegetable farm
near Falmouth, Massachusetts.
Just got the first cow they
ever had, of which they are
very proud. Mr. Andrews
works as a day laborer at a
nearby army camp. FSA
clients. Falmouth, Massachusetts. December 1940.

*Russell Lee*

Mexican pecan workers
waiting at Union Hall for
assignment to work. San Antonio, Texas. March 1939.

*23*

Marion Post Wolcott

Copper miners on strike
waiting for scabs to come out
of mines. Ducktown, Tennessee. October 1939.

24

*Marion Post Wolcott*

Coal miners. The "lady's
man" and "smart guy."
Bertha Hill, West Virginia.
September 1938.

*John Vachon*

Picket line at the King Farm
strike. Near Morrisville,
Pennsylvania. August 1938.

*Dorothea Lange*

Speaker, migratory worker,
leader in the cotton strike, at
Conference to Aid Agricultural Organization, saying,
"Brother, hit's pick 75¢
cotton or starve. Brother,
hit's pick 75¢ cotton or else."
Bakersfield, California. 1938.

27

*Dorothea Lange*

Grandmother from Oklahoma
and her pieced quilt. Kern
County, California. February
1936.

*28*

*Dorothea Lange*

Street meeting at night in
Mexican town outside of
Shafter, California. Organizer
for United Cannery, Agricultural, Packing and Allied
Workers of America (CIO)
talks to mixed crowd. The
strike failed. Shafter, California. November 1938.

*Dorothea Lange*

He came from an Oklahoma farm in April 1938. Became a migratory farm worker in California, joined the United Agricultural, Packing and Allied Workers of America (CIO) at the beginning of the cotton strike of October 1938, and became the leader of the "Flying Squadron" which attempted to picket the large fields of corporation farms by automobile caravans. He drove the first car. Kern County, California. November 1938.

*Dorothea Lange*

Housing for Oklahoma refugees in California. February 1936.

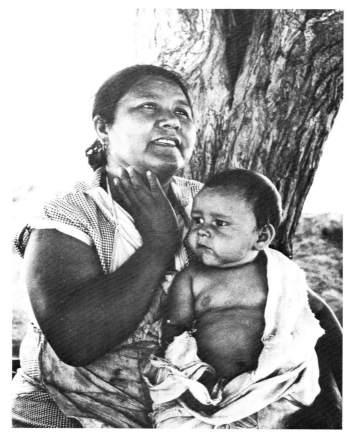

*Dorothea Lange*

Mexican mother in California. "Sometimes I tell my children that I would like to go to Mexico, but they tell me, 'We don't want to go; we belong here.' " June 1935.

*Dorothea Lange*

Negro field worker has just
made himself some shoes out
of that old tire. Holtville,
Imperial Valley, California.
June 1935.

33

*Dorothea Lange*

Children of migratory carrot pullers, Mexicans, in the Imperial Valley, California. March 1937.

34

*Dorothea Lange*

Japanese mother and daughter, agricultural workers. Near Guadalupe, California. March 1937.

*Arthur Rothstein*

Exhibit at Grand Central Station. New York City, New York. 1943.

# Command Performances:

*Photography from the United States Department of Agriculture*

## Pete Daniel

Since its inception as a bureau during the Civil War, the United States Department of Agriculture (USDA) has dispensed information to farmers. Drawing on scholarship from land-grant colleges, set up in the Morrill Act of 1862, and from experiment stations, sanctioned in the Hatch Act of 1877, the USDA published pamphlets and bulletins that suggested better farming practices. The Federal Extension Service, begun in 1902, carried the gospel of better farming techniques directly to rural people. In 1914 Congress formalized the agency, and three years later it voted for grants to incorporate agricultural education in high school curriculums. By 1930 these federal, state, and local institutions had a large national constituency, and thus, from every angle, farmers heard the same advice—forsake the old ways and modernize. Photographs became a crucial tool in transmitting images of progress.[1]

Millions of farmers, however, lacked the necessary opportunity, finances, or literacy to utilize the progressive notions pouring from the USDA. Committed to common sense and traditional methods of husbandry, many distrusted both the government and the new emphasis on scientific research. Recent historical scholarship has debated the role of the federal agricultural complex on the development of farm life. While few deny that government action was desperately needed in 1933—to reduce a massive surplus, raise prices, and stabilize production—many question the methods used and the purposes served, especially when human costs are tallied against economic and political considerations. Such questions are crucial because the structure of agriculture changed drastically in the 1930s: within a generation

large farm operations increased, sharecropping practically disappeared, and mechanization and science came to dominate the countryside.[2]

The photographs the USDA commissioned to portray this transformation were scarcely neutral. Typically, they presented one of three scenarios. Some portrayed farmers as stable and prosperous, as if there were no hint of discontent across rural America. Others, depicting the increasing role of government in peoples' lives, featured benevolent personnel eager to pass on the benefits of federal programs. Still others illustrated how the miracles of science and technology could both relieve farmers of drudgery and produce better crop yields. On the whole, the USDA photographs showed the department maintaining rural traditions while simultaneously serving as the agent of transformation.

When President Franklin D. Roosevelt offered a New Deal to the American people in March 1933, farmers listened attentively. Despite long-standing misgivings about government intervention, they were desperate enough to try any plan that promised recovery. Passed in the spring of 1933, the Agricultural Adjustment Act radically changed the federal role in agriculture by regulating how much farmers could produce through an allotment system. The Agricultural Adjustment Administration (AAA) supported farmers by paying them to reduce acreage (thus curtailing the surplus that drove down prices) and by guaranteeing higher prices for the crops farmers did produce.

In expanding the federal role in agriculture beyond its traditional educational function, the AAA set in motion forces that reduced the number of farmers and altered their relationship to the land. The concentration of land into fewer hands, a trend that had been in progress since the Civil War, accelerated, and the number of farms dwindled from a high of 6.8 million in 1935 to roughly 2.3 million today. During this half century, a revolution occurred in farm structure as mechanization, the application of chemicals, and federal programs transformed agriculture from a labor-intensive to a capital-intensive enterprise. The AAA effectively directed agricultural policy in the thirties, and it attempted to explain New Deal programs and win support from both farmers and the public at large.

In general New Deal agricultural policies operated in a friendly environment. "Publicity is already favorable," Milton S. Eisenhower, director of information for the USDA, observed in the fall of 1933. "This administration has a friendlier press than any since the war." Still he realized that some people complained about farm programs and distrusted government intervention. Consequently, the USDA generated press releases, radio talks, publications, and photographs that championed the role of government in rural America.[3]

By the mid-thirties, the USDA bureaucracy employed hundreds of people to generate its publicity. The department published nine periodicals, including *Extension Service Review, Soil Conservation, Journal of Agricultural Research,* and *Experiment Station Record.* Photographs were a crucial part of this information campaign and many appeared in government publications. The USDA files, however, were also open to commercial periodical and book publishers. In 1935, for example, an Allyn and Bacon editor requested ten photographs to illustrate a book on health, and a year later an editor at Charles Scribner's ordered sixteen photographs of livestock, crops, and county agent activities for twenty cents each. The USDA collection of twenty-three thousand photographs, now housed in the National Archives, contains images from the AAA, the Federal Extension Service, the Forest Service, the Soil Conservation Service, the Rural Electrification Administration (REA), the Civilian Conservation Corps (CCC), among other agencies.[4]

Of the two dozen photographers who worked for the USDA's various agencies, George W. Ackerman left an exceptional legacy, and his career at the Federal Extension Service provides insight into the work of a government photographer. Born in Baltimore in 1884, Ackerman moved to Washington in 1910 and took a job as a photographer with the Bureau of Plant Industry. In 1917 the Federal Extension Service hired him for $900 per year. During his tenure at the agency, which lasted through the 1940s, Ackerman visited all forty-eight states and, according to his calculations, took more than fifty thousand photographs "depicting all phases of rural life." He also instructed local agents in photography. His photographs appeared in such government publications as *Extension Service Review* and the *Agricultural Yearbook,* but many of his images, whether in government or commercial publications, carried no credit line.

Ackerman recalled that when he started his career most photographs of rural America were "either of the nostalgic, old-oaken-bucket type or the hayseed making-fun-of-farm-life type." His goal was "to paint the rural scene as I saw it, modern and up-to-date in many respects." His well-composed photographs show a hard-working and proud rural America. "My pictures have all been made to point to a better way of life for rural people," he recalled. "I have neither specialized in the sordid nor glamor[ous] but in the everyday things sometimes beautiful, sometimes humorous."[5]

Ackerman's subject matter was defined by the Visual Instruction and Editorial Section of the Extension Service, which shared his expenses with state extension departments.[6] A typical trip, such as the one he took in the summer of 1935, routed him to Oklahoma, Arkansas, Georgia, Florida, Mississippi, and Alabama. Lester A. Schlup, who headed the section, suggested that in addition to other subjects "it might be desirable to get a few pictures of negro women making quilts and mattresses." L. O. Brackeen, the extension editor in Alabama, thought that Ackerman should cover "recreation activities, home improvement, organization work, mares with mule colts, club boys with their pigs, calves and farm products, cotton being harvested, marketed, stored, etc., and a number of individual success stories."[7] Writing to the agent in Anniston, Alabama, Brackeen insisted that Ackerman "make a number of pictures on farms of two or three of the most successful farmers in the county."[8] Such assignments led to images of a narrow slice of rural life. Indeed, in the USDA holdings there are but ten photographs in the "Farm Houses—Tenant" file. Three of these were borrowed from Farm Security Administration (FSA) files, and the other seven show homes of prosperous tenants.

Ackerman's images primarily depict thriving farmers who employ the latest information from the USDA, use modern implements, own good specimens of livestock, and live in comfortable homes. Above all, they picture contented farmers. Youngsters pose with their prize livestock or at agricultural demonstrations. Women feed chickens, can food, tend gardens, milk, sew, and iron, while men work in the fields. Predictably, the Extension Service files portrayed "the most successful farmers," neglecting struggling tenant farmers or the hardships of rural life. The images mirror the fact that the programs administered by the service largely bypassed sharecroppers and tenants.[9] Ackerman's view of rural America was prescribed by his position as agency photographer.

In an April 1933 trip through Louisiana, for example, Ackerman concentrated on black farmers because his supervisor observed that "our file of this phase of extension activities is very inadequate."[10] In St. Landry Parish, Louisiana, Ackerman did a series of photographs of blacks. In one, a group of black farmers, several apparently dressed in their Sunday best, gathered around the white extension specialist, fully absorbed in the demonstration (fig. 36). Butchering pork, of course, was an integral part of rural life, but not a chore that required Sunday clothes; it was a command performance.

Most USDA photographs of rural blacks depict them in such poses, usually listening to a white agent. These are hardly images of the harsh and impoverished reality that defined the farm life of most rural blacks. Such photographs, however, were useful to the Extension Service, for they showed that government funds were used to instruct blacks as well as whites. By the 1930s there were hundreds of black extension and home demonstration agents, but these workers were strictly supervised by whites and black extension work, in general, was never a priority of the agency. The photographs of black extension workers reflect the separate and unequal status of blacks throughout the South.

Ackerman's April 1933 photograph of an open-air basketball game in Jacksonville, Texas, provides a rare view of organized recreation in the black community (fig. 37). Throughout the rural South most sports events were held outdoors well into the thirties, as neither blacks nor whites had suitable athletic or educational facilities.[11] Using the limited sources at hand, these blacks enjoyed a game of basketball, and Ackerman was on hand to capture an image of the more pleasant side of rural life.

By the summer of 1933, New Deal relief agencies extended aid. A few of the early programs, such as the Federal Emergency Relief Administration (FERA), provided direct relief to some people while rehabilitating others by placing them on farms. Although most unemployed people were willing to work, there simply were not enough jobs.[12] Ackerman found eight black women, apparently on relief, shucking corn beside a dump truck near Durham, North Carolina (fig. 38). Such federal cooperative canning centers, which helped rural people preserve food for the winter months, attracted many USDA photographers. Yet despite such programs as the FERA, the Civil Works Administration, and the WPA, many rural people never recovered their economic health but instead either became more dependent on government programs or moved about the country searching for jobs and opportunity.

Other USDA photographers also contributed to the file on black farmers. O. S. Welch's 1939 photograph of poor black children in Alabama is exceptional in a collection dominated by images of prosperous members of the black community (fig. 39). In both the photograph and the caption milk is emphasized because it suggested that even in such a poor environment there was hope for better nourishment and, ultimately, a better life. It is unclear if the milk came from the family's cow or from a government program. The caption to this photograph, unlike most relating to blacks, gives the names of the subjects, perhaps an indication that by 1939 blacks were receiving more equal treatment from the USDA, at least in agency publicity.

L. C. Harmon's 1940 photograph of black students attending a farm management class at Tuskegee Institute reflects the paradox of agricultural education stressing mechanization in the face of rural depression and dispossession (fig. 40). The wall posters advertise machines that represent modernization, the same machines that would drastically change Alabama agriculture within a generation. Yet most of these young men never had the resources to purchase the implements that revolutionized farm life. Indeed, owing largely to mechanization and discriminatory government programs, black farmers have all but disappeared from the rural landscape.

Millions of whites also left rural America during the Depression, and some of the decade's most poignant photographs, especially those from the FSA, capture migrants in search of new opportunities. Ackerman's 1933 photograph of a well-dressed young Maryland man leaving home to seek work in a city contrasts sharply with FSA images of desperate farmers fleeing rural areas in broken-down cars (fig. 41). The caption does not explain why the young man is leaving or why he travels without luggage. Apparently, his trip was not the forced march of many of the country's migrants; he is simply a rural youth leaving home to seek his fortune.

Even as New Deal agencies confronted the depression crisis in rural America, Ackerman's images captured a sense of stability rather than upheaval. In Vermont in 1938 he found a roadside market with bountiful apples, pears, and cider (fig. 42). Even farmers who were not turning to mechanization appeared vigorous and stable, as shown in the 1939 photograph of a Nevada farmer cutting barley (fig. 43). In his photograph of agent T. E. Buckman talking with a farmer, the farmer has proudly nailed his Farm Bureau membership plaque to the gate, while the agent's car advertises the USDA, the Farm Bureau, and the University of Nevada (fig. 44). In Montana, during the same trip, Ackerman posed state extension editor, Louis True, with farmer S. Bloom. The grain has been cut and stacked in shocks, and a leisurely air of well-being pervades the scene (fig. 45). In none of these four photographs does any hint of depression emerge. Yet in Missouri in 1939, hundreds of sharecroppers, displaced from their farms, were camping beside the road, a protest necessitated by the USDA's refusal to enforce planter's contracts that would keep tenants on the land.[13]

By presenting a positive image that stressed recovery and stability, the USDA avoided dealing with some of the serious problems set in motion by the Depression and by agency policies. The dignified but clearly run-down conditions surrounding the eight black women in Durham County (fig. 38) contrasts sharply with Ackerman's photograph of Ilene Holder, taken in Mississippi in 1935 (fig. 46). Well-dressed, attractive, and self-confident, Holder stands behind the utensils of home canning, ready to demonstrate the process. She personifies the ideal of the 4-H Club and, by extension, the USDA's insistence that its programs would reshape farm life in this image.

The photograph of Holder appeared in the January 1936 issue of *Extension Service Review* along with director C. W. Warburton's article urging an expanded extension program. Warburton wrote that the Extension Service had received supplemental appropriations of $8 million that would permit hiring 1,250 new workers. Extension, Warburton argued, should be involved in an increasing spectrum of farm programs: "Farm credit, soil conservation, rural rehabilitation, rural electrification, all of them offer a service of vital interest to farm families and belong in an extension program."[14]

Some agencies, such as the Rural Electrification Administration (REA), requested aid from extension workers, for they also sought to improve rural life. Primitive conditions prevailed on most of the country's seven million farms during the thirties, not just because most farm work was labor-intensive but also because three-fourths of the rural population lacked indoor plumbing and 90 percent had no electricity. Established in 1935, the REA provided federal expertise, but it relied on local enthusiasm to form cooperatives. For a five dollar fee, a farmer could join a cooperative and qualify for loans to install power lines that could be paid off over a twenty-five year period. Farmers eagerly formed cooperatives, convinced neighbors to join, and impatiently awaited the day when the lines would be energized. Because farm women realized that electricity could bring running water, indoor plumbing, electric stoves and irons, and refrigerators, in many instances they led the crusade for power.[15]

To spread its message, the REA started a newsletter in 1935 that quickly turned into the magazine *Rural Electrification News*. In 1939, the REA found a permanent home within the USDA. The agency never concentrated on securing quality photographs, relying instead on snapshots, often by local photographers. Still the holdings of the REA and the USDA photographic files in the National Archives contain numerous examples of the impact of electricity on farm life; these depict not only line construction but also the work routine of women before and after electricity arrived. Other photographs record the institutional impact of REA. An REA truck bears witness to the agency's presence in New York (fig. 47); the co-op building in Louisiana is probably a symbol of pride (fig. 48). Country people took pride in obtaining electric service, for it not only eased chores but brought conveniences formerly available only to urbanites. The REA epitomized the thrust of the New Deal that challenged big business, for it demonstrated that a cooperative movement aided by the federal government could furnish electricity.

Although New Deal agencies such as the WPA, CCC, and the National Youth Administration (NYA), were phased out early in the war, the AAA has continued to formulate agricultural policy. Whatever the impact of other agencies, the AAA clearly transformed the life of the country's farmers, for the government dictated planting decisions, provided credit, established conservation programs, and set the larger agenda for rural Americans. The USDA supported farmers who listened attentively to Extension Service advice, read USDA bulletins, and employed the latest ideas, for nearly all USDA programs were directed at farmers who could adopt science and technology. Those who scorned the agency's notion of progress were neglected, along with millions of tenants, sharecroppers, and wage laborers—the bottom rung of the agricultural ladder. While some agencies, such as the FSA, helped poorer farmers, it would not be unfair to conclude that they were largely ignored by USDA programs.[16]

The Extension Service, as well as other federal agencies dealing with rural America, approached its tasks with the best intentions. It was, after all, an era of active government involvement. Those who extended government programs to farmers saw benefits pouring into the countryside. USDA photographers recorded such benefits, but that was only one part of the picture. There was another view of the thirties, of rural America, that was beyond the focal length of USDA lenses.

The idyllic images of rural life that typified most USDA photographs extended into portrayals of New Deal programs, with only an occasional hint of ambivalence or dissatisfaction. The photographs that follow demonstrate how the AAA informed farmers of its programs, held referendums, controlled production, distributed payments, and kept records.

In August 1933, Ackerman visited Utah, and near Clarkston he photographed a county agent explaining the wheat allotment plan to a group of farmers (fig. 49). A similar photograph ran in the *Extension Service Review* a month later (fig. 50). By this time extension agents, no longer confining their activities to education alone, had become spokesmen for federal policy. The further the USDA strayed from its traditional role the more it relied upon radio, periodicals, and photographs to translate its new powers.

Since farmers voted on the government programs,

the AAA stressed that its policies were voluntary. In fact, farmers had only two options—to vote for the program of crop reduction and then collect benefit payments for cooperation, or to take their chances on supply and demand. Most voted for the programs. Photographer J. T. Mitchell posed a black farmer in Pulaski County, Arkansas, in 1938, casting a vote in a cotton referendum (fig. 51). While many black sharecroppers and tenants (and eventually landowners) left agriculture in part because of the AAA programs, by voting in AAA referendums they got their first taste of democratic participation.[17] By insisting on the participation of black farmers, the AAA subtly challenged southern disfranchisement laws.

When farmers voted to reduce crop acreage, government workers measured fields to ensure compliance. Ackerman found a measuring crew in Lauderdale County, Mississippi, in 1934, checking on cotton acreage (fig. 52). As the government payments for compliance provided farmers with needed cash, many reluctantly adapted to having the USDA direct their planting decisions. In another photograph, taken in Kaufman County, Texas, in 1934, Ackerman captured the payoff for farming with the government as farmers file along to receive their benefit checks (fig. 53). The image may suggest a hint of dissatisfaction—at least in the puzzled look of the farmer in the foreground—but the photograph, when published along with several other USDA images, told only part of the story (fig. 54). The FSA, serving a different constituency, showed another, that of displacement, migration, and forced resettlement.

To provide accurate statistics on farmers, a large staff of women clerks labored over calculators and tally sheets. Every farm in the country was in a government file. Figure 55 presents a sanitized view of bureaucracy, but many farmers complained about red tape, about the loss of independence, about programs that provided no flexibility for exceptional cases, and especially about allotments being reduced below the acreage needed to survive. The impact of AAA programs was uneven. Larger farmers, with more land to manipulate, fared better than small landowners. Sharecroppers, although in theory protected from capricious landlords, often received less than their fair share of government proceeds. Some landlords cheated their tenants and in many cases, especially in the cotton area, simply dismissed unneeded workers.

By the mid-thirties USDA photographers not only documented AAA programs but increasingly recorded indications of mechanization and the impact of science. It was as if the idea of progress had at last caught on in rural America. Yet progress had its costs. Landowners, for example, often took their government payments and invested in machinery, which idled even more farm workers. One posed 1939 shot of a farmer with a tractor salesman graphically illustrated the benefits to be gained from government programs (fig. 56). Mechanization of farm tasks increased and was portrayed as progress, but it came at the expense of sharecroppers and less prosperous landowners.[18]

Along with machine technology, as epitomized by tractors, scientific research led to sweeping changes in the structure of farming. By the late 1930s, government scientists were concentrating on chemicals to control insects and other pests. A decade later herbicides were developed that, in effect, chopped out the weeds, freeing hired workers from the task and once again reducing the rural work force. William Forsyth's 1941 photograph shows an army of men—advancing on Mormon crickets—with labor-intensive hand-spraying equipment (fig. 57), but aerial technology was already in the experimental stage. A 1937 photograph depicts an Autogiro spraying a Florida test plot, a precursor of crop dusting that became common after the war (fig. 58). Science and technology were thus joined in creating a revolution in rural work routines.

By the late 1930s, USDA photographs documented numerous experiments that demonstrated the use of science and chemistry—not a new trend, but one that assumed increasing importance. Forsythe found Mary Logan carefully weighing a rat in 1941, calculating how to improve human nutrition by studying the rodent's eating habits (fig. 59).

In contrast to his usual subject matter, George W. Ackerman's 1941 photograph of a chicken packing plant in Maryland offers a radical departure from the bucolic images that are his legacy (fig. 60). The mechanized line of broilers and harried workers defies his usually placid compositions. The plucked broilers eclipse the workers, showing vividly the structural change from the chicken coop and the casual barnyard feeding to the regulated assembly line. Intended or not, this photograph, taken by a master of composition who typically flattered farm workers, is a document of the changes quickly spreading through United States agriculture. Whether one looked to the broiler industry, or to cotton, rice, or hogs, American agriculture was moving from labor-intensive to capital-intensive operations, from small to large farms, from a way of life to a way of business.

A well-composed shot taken in July 1939 at the USDA Beltsville farm near Washington is a more subtle document of federal agricultural policy (fig. 61). Despite the lengthy caption, it is not clear why bulls needed exercise, why such an elaborate ring was necessary, or why a hired hand kept them all moving with his whip. Yet the closed circle that the bulls plod around is a perfect symbol of the entropy introduced by USDA policies. Only farmers who had allotments could plant cash crops, and in most commodity areas only landowners had allotments. Agriculture became a closed occupation, for in most instances only those who were already involved in farming could follow that way of life. The spirit of independence, of trial and error, of husbandry as a way of life and not a way to profit, of community support faded. Instead of looking to nature and traditional husbandry, those who survived the lean years looked to science, technology, and federal planners.

The USDA photographs of prosperous farmers functioned much like advertisements showing how farmers should look and how they should look up to government. The government always appeared as a friendly advisor, and the changes it introduced were best. When footnoted by historical research and the quite different images of FSA photographers, however, the USDA photographs assume another context, one in which the contradictions between the stated goals of federal planners and the reality of farm life emerge. In focusing on a bucolic rural America, they indireclty showed the seeds of change—the federal programs, the machines, the science. But the publicity effort did not deal directly with the human costs of this revolutionary shift in policy or reveal the full impact of the Depression. One reason that the Farm Security Administration photographs became so controversial in the late 1930s is that they did show the human dimensions of a transformation that would reduce the nation's farms so drastically. The photograph file of the USDA raises serious questions about the government's use of images to further its goals. Given the ongoing record of dispossession since the thirties and the present crisis in American agriculture, these "official images" suggest a different story altogether.

# Notes

1. See Alan I. Marcus, *Agricultural Science and the Quest for Legitimacy: Farmers, Agricultural Colleges, and Experiment Stations, 1870–1890* (Ames, 1985); Roy V. Scott, *The Reluctant Farmer: The Rise of Agricultural Extension to 1914* (Urbana, 1970); Alfred Charles True, *A History of Agricultural Education in the United States, 1785–1925* (Washington, 1929); Pete Daniel, *Breaking the Land: The Transformation of Cotton, Tobacco, and Rice Cultures since 1880* (Urbana, 1985), 6–18; John T. Schlebecker, *Whereby We Thrive: A History of American Farming, 1607–1972* (Ames, 1975); Gilbert C. Fite, *Cotton Fields No More: Southern Agriculture, 1865–1980* (Lexington, 1984).

2. See *Structure Issues in American Agriculture*, USDA, ESCS, Agricultural Economic Report 438 (November 1979); *Changing Character and Structure of American Agriculture: An Overview*, U.S. General Accounting Office (September 1978). The best introduction to the issues can be found in Jack Temple Kirby, *Rural Worlds Lost: The American South, 1920–1960* (Baton Rouge, 1987); Daniel, *Breaking the Land;* and Fite, *Cotton Fields No More*.

3. Milton S. Eisenhower, undated memorandum (probably November 1933) to Paul Appleby, General Correspondence, Publicity, Records of the Secretary of Agriculture, Record Group 16, National Archives (hereafter cited as SOA, RG 16, NA).

4. S. Elizabeth Vevoy to N. P. Tucker, May 25, 1936; Laura S. Johnson to Visual Instruction Section, July 11, 1935, Central Files, 1935–36, Washington, D. C., Records of the Federal Extension Service, Record Group 33, National Archives (hereafter cited as Extension Service, RG 33, NA): Henry A. Wallace to J. Parnell Thomas, June 2, 1938, General Correspondence, Publicity, SOA, RG 16, NA.

5. Clara Ackerman to Diane Hamilton, May 7, 1974; autobiographical sketch; and personnel record, all in possession of Diane Hamilton. Ackerman's photographs are contained in the USDA file, Still Pictures Division, SOA RG 16, NA.

6. "States Cooperate in Photographic Work," *Extension Service Review* 1 (October 1930), 96; L. A. Schlup to L. O. Brackeen, April 27, 1935, General Correspondence, Alabama, Extension Service, RG 33, NA.

7. Schlup to Brackeen, July 17, 1935, General Correspondence, Alabama, Extension Service, RG 33, NA; Brackeen to Lester Schlup, July 13, 1935.

8. Brackeen to S. R. Doughty, August 6, 1935, Extension Service, RG 33, NA.

9. Gilbert Fite, *Cotton Fields No More*, 224; Daniel, *Breaking the Land*, 104.

10. Ruben Brigham to C. B. Smith, April 4, 1933, General Correspondence, Alabama, Extension Service, RG 33, NA. Thomas M. Campbell, head of black extension workers, coordinated Ackerman's assignment to photograph blacks. See Campbell to Brigham, March 24, 1933, Extension Service, RG 33, NA.

11. Pete Daniel, *Standing at the Crossroads: Southern Life Since 1900* (New York, 1986), 8.

12. Philip G. Beck and M. C. Foster, *Six Rural Problem Areas: Relief—Resources—Rehabilitation: An Analysis of the Human and Material Resources in Six Rural Areas with High Relief Rates*, Research Monograph 1 (Washington, 1935); John A. Salmond, *A Southern Rebel: The Life and Times of Aubrey Willis Williams, 1890–1965* (Chapel Hill, 1983).

13. Louis Cantor, *A Prologue to the Protest Movement: The Missouri Sharecropper Roadside Demonstration of 1939* (Durham 1969); Donald H. Grubbs, *Cry from the Cotton: The Southern Tenant Farmers' Union and the New Deal* (Chapel Hill, 1971).

14. *Extension Service Review* 7 (January 1936), 8.

15. Richard A. Pence, ed., *The Next Greatest Thing* (Washington, 1984); Morris L. Cooke, "Electrify the Farm," *Today* (June 18, 1935), 6–7, copy in Morris L. Cooke file, Records of the Rural Electrification Administration, Record Group 221, National Archives; Udo Rall, "The REA Program and the Extension Service," June 3, 1941, manuscript in Information Services Division, Office Files of Udo Rall, Record Group 221, National Archives.

16. Interview with Paul Appleby, 1952–53, Columbia University Oral History Project, 97–98, copy in Library of Congress. See also, Calvin Hoover, memorandum to the Secretary of Agriculture, January 8, 1935, Landlord Tenant File, Records of the Agricultural Adjustment Administration, Record Group 45, National Archives.

17. Anthony J. Badger, *Prosperity Road: The New Deal, Tobacco, and North Carolina* (Chapel Hill, 1980), 225–27.

18. Daniel, *Breaking the Land*, 168–83.

36

*George W. Ackerman*

Extension specialist outlining
demonstration in meat
cutting. St. Landry Parish,
Louisiana. April 1933.

37

*George W. Ackerman*

Negro community spring
meeting, recreation. Jacksonville, Texas. April 1933.

*38*

*George W. Ackerman*

Preparing corn for canning at
the community canning plant
for relief. This garden was on
the county home farm. Durham County, North Carolina.
September 1933.

*39*

*O. S. Welch*

Korine Kelly, Sada Lee Kelly,
and Mary Kelly drinking
milk. Children of Hestella
Kelly. Route #2, Greensboro,
Alabama.

*40*

*L. C. Harmon*

Junior class in farm management at Tuskegee Institute. May 10, 1940.

41

*George W. Ackerman*

Farm boy leaving home to go
to the city to work. Frederick
County, Maryland. Novem-
ber 1933.

42

*George W. Ackerman*

A roadside market stand.
Ferrisburg, Chittenden
County, Vermont. September
1938.

*43*

*George W. Ackerman*

Harvesting Trebi barley.
Douglas County, Nevada.
July 1939.

*44*

*George W. Ackerman*

Farmer Louis Fafetto and
T. E. Buckman, assistant
director of Extension, reviewing Extension and Farm
Bureau programs of the past
twenty years. Nevada. July
1939.

45

*George W. Ackerman*

Montana Extension editor,
Louis True, gets his story in
S. Bloom's oat field. Mon-
tana. July 1939.

46

*George W. Ackerman*

Four-H Club member Ilene
Holder prepared to give a
canning demonstration.
Holmes County, Mississippi.
August 1935.

47

*George W. Ackerman*

One of the first electric lines
to be constructed with
R.E.A. funds is a single phase
line and the extension is 6.54
miles long and serves twenty
customers. Cayuga County,
New York. August 1938.

*48*

*Peter Sakaer*

R.E.A. co-op office. Lafay-
ette, Louisiana. 1939.

*George W. Ackerman*

County agent holding wheat
meeting explaining Federal
wheat allotment plan. Clarkston, Cache County, Utah.
August 1933.

[A photograph similar to figure 49, published in *Extension Service Review,* October 1933, 87.]

## Last-Minute Extension Views

*J. T. Mitchell*

A Pulaski County, Arkansas, cotton grower drops his ballot in the cotton marketing quota referendum held December 10, 1938.

52

*George W. Ackerman*

Local measuring crew measuring land in cotton and the rented acres. Lauderdale County, Mississippi. July 1934.

53

*George W. Ackerman*

Farmers receiving benefit
checks. Kaufman County,
Texas. July 1934.

[Photograph from figure 53 as it appeared in *Extension Service Review,* December 1934, 185.]

# Along the Highways and Byways of Adjustment

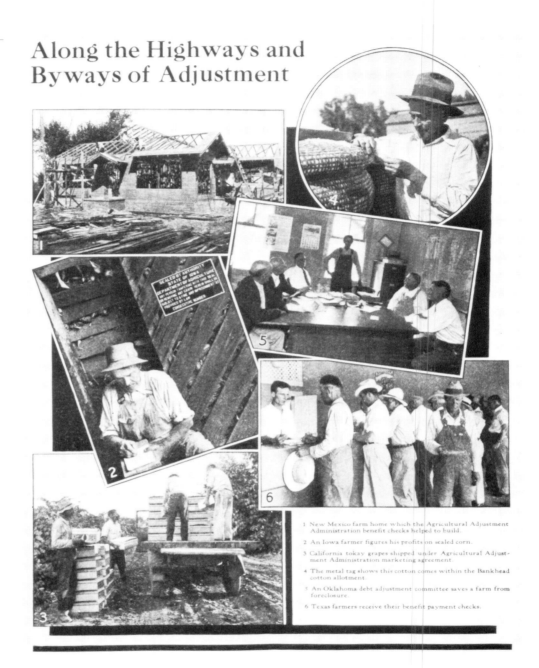

1 New Mexico farm home which the Agricultural Adjustment Administration benefit checks helped to build.

2 An Iowa farmer figures his profits on scaled corn.

3 California tokay grapes shipped under Agricultural Adjustment Administration marketing agreement.

4 The metal tag shows this cotton comes within the Bankhead cotton allotment.

5 An Oklahoma debt adjustment committee saves a farm from foreclosure.

6 Texas farmers receive their benefit payment checks.

*George W. Ackerman*

Summary of performance forms are compared with the listing sheets in the statistical section. Dodge County, Nebraska. August 1938.

*Peter Killian*

Cutting supplies of apples down to the market demand for them, under the Federal Surplus Purchase Plan, helps stabilize prices, in some instances keeping them high enough to return a small profit to the grower. Farmers saved from going into the red on their apple crop may at least look into the possibility of buying new tools. 1939.

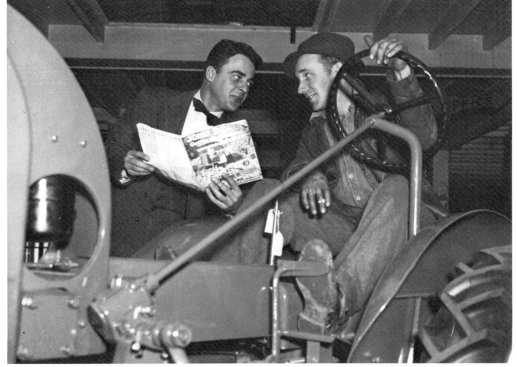

*William Forsyth*

A hand-dusting crew advances on a band of migrating crickets. June 1941.

Autogiro in test spraying paris green. One line of pans may be seen just in front of plane. Sanford, Florida. April 1, 1937.

*William Forsyth*

Miss Mary Logan, nutrition worker in the U.S. Department of Agriculture, records the weight of a rat living on an adequate diet. The way laboratory rats respond to various diets is a guide to the way human beings will respond to the right food. 1941.

60

*George W. Ackerman*

Dressing line for 3-pound
broilers at the Agar Corporation dressing plant. Berlin,
Worcester County, Maryland.
September 1941.

Bulls of the U.S. Department of Agriculture's experimental dairy herd at the Beltsville Research Center walk around a ring for an hour and a half each day. This exercise tones their muscles and keeps them in top physical condition. Two bulls pull the "merry-go-round" with yoke and singletrees. The other bulls just plod along. The man on the platform keeps the bulls moving. July 1939.

# Publicity, Husbandry, and Technocracy

*Fact and Symbol in Civilian Conservation Corps Photography*

## Maren Stange

The Civilian Conservation Corps (CCC) was the first of the New Deal relief agencies put in place in response to the crises of the Great Depression. Acclaimed from its inception in 1933 as the president's "pet project" and said to bear his "personal stamp," "Roosevelt's Tree Army" sought to fulfill a dual purpose: to relieve and rehabilitate unemployed young men and at the same time conserve and replenish forests, parks, and farmlands long neglected and exploited.[1] Until the threat of war in Europe forced a shift in CCC priorities in 1939, enrollees, assigned to Army-administered camps located throughout the states, territories, and island possessions, worked an eight-hour day on projects directed by agencies in the departments of Agriculture and the Interior. They planted trees and built roads, bridges, truck trails, telephone lines, and fire lookout towers; they restored and preserved historical sites and monuments and improved national and state forests and parks; they aided farmers in soil conservation, water development, and improvement of western grazing lands; they worked on flood control in the Northeast and helped implement a major wildlife restoration program throughout the country. Experienced firefighters available at a moment's notice, enrollees stood ready to assist in floods, tornadoes, and other emergencies.[2]

The agency's transformative purposes and effects, in regard to both human and natural resources, were "easily perceivable," as historian John Salmond has written, and so were the material and social gains CCC work offered to country and community. Supplementing its appealingly romantic imagery (see figs. 62–65), statistics

helped to point out the benefits: more than half the forest planting in the history of the nation was done by the CCC; by 1938 enrollees had planted more than 200 million trees on soil conservation projects; by 1942 the Corps had spent nearly 6.5 million days fighting fires; and the average enrollee gained eight to fourteen pounds in weight and one half inch in height while in camp.[3]

Indeed, the CCC easily attracted public interest and acclaim, thereby obviating the elaborate public relations efforts necessarily undertaken by later, more controversial agencies. Thus, of the approximately ten thousand photographs of CCC activities held in the National Archives, only a small proportion were made by a professional photographer. For most of its existence, the agency used photographs made by officials of the Agriculture, Labor, Interior, and War departments, which cooperated in the CCC's administration, and by foresters, soil conservationists, Army officers, and CCC enrollees themselves. Central offices in Washington relied on workers in the field for "good live CCC photographs" and "shots with timely news interest," and they instituted only the most haphazard scheme for distributing such images (when they appeared) to local and national publications.[4]

By the time of its abolition in 1942, the CCC had attracted more than 2.5 million men.[5] They were, for the most part, single, between seventeen and twenty-five years of age, unemployed, and from families on relief, to whom they were required to send a substantial percentage of the $30 per month wages. Not surprisingly, young men were hard hit by the Depression: 25 percent of those between fourteen and twenty-four were unemployed and nearly 30 percent had found only part-time work;[6] education was scanty for most in lower income groups. Every kind of disadvantage or lack of opportunity was intensified for blacks,[7] whose unemployment rates stood at double the national average.[8] Those who came to the camps had become "desperate and rootless," George Rawick claims.[9] For most enrollees, Salmond notes, "enlistment in the CCC had been the final act, the culmination of a long period of despair and helplessness" at the failure to find work and the transience, family suffering, and social dislocation that resulted.[10]

What enrollees turned to, as these photographs suggest, was an organization that seemed to renew—in the midst of industrial depression—a time-honored vision of America as a bucolic "middle landscape," an "undefiled, green republic, a quiet land of forests, villages, and farms dedicated to the pursuit of happiness," as literary historian Leo Marx describes it.[11] The prospect of young men at work in the continent's forests and farmlands seemed to confirm a version of history that cast the Anglo-Saxon settlement of North America as the rightful establishment of an "agrarian empire" to be built and husbanded by a "pioneer army." Such a "Garden of the World" had figured from the beginning of national ideology; it seemed the sure source of national wealth and the preservation of self-sufficiency, happiness, dignity, and honor in the "American race."[12] Seeming to embody the values of a simpler, earlier time, CCC work promised recruits not only the chance to prove themselves (and their worth to the nation) in the wilderness just like those who first settled and exploited the frontier, but also the opportunity to claim for their own the special virtues agrarian myth had long attributed to those who live by cultivating the soil.

Despite or perhaps because of the agency's reliance on nonprofessionals, CCC publicity readily deployed the cultural symbols that connoted pastoralism for an audience already accustomed to the mass media. "Had we taken pictures of a group of CCC boys standing near the statue which was built to Paul Bunyan, reproduced in LIFE in a recent issue, we would probably have obtained some nation-wide publicity on it," lamented Guy McKinney, chief of the Division of Public Relations, to an associate in 1937. Nevertheless, he concluded, a picture of "a CCC truck full of enrollees taking a look at

their heroic predecessor" might be "worthwhile." Three years later, McKinney received an elaborate proposal from Granville E. Dickey, a CCC official involved with the "recreated Lincoln Village" at New Salem, Illinois, concerning a way to "get something which will suggest the spirit of Lincoln as typified by the modern CCC boy." This will be particularly true," Dickey continued, "if there are several very tall and gaunt youngsters at the New Salem camp," some of whom, he hoped, might be photographed "splitting rails" or engaged in other activities similar to those shown in the film *Young Mr. Lincoln.* "I think we might also employ photomontage or double printing to strip in an actual photograph of Lincoln as a background on some of the shots made," Dickey added, anxious that the historical connections he proposed be made perfectly clear.[13]

Less blatant than these attempts to exploit both popular culture and familiar folkloric icons, the photographs reproduced as figures 66, 67, and 68 nevertheless depend on a representative set of cultural symbols. The crowd of urbanites in figure 66 appeared in the first issue of *Happy Days,* the official CCC newspaper.[14] Their flashlit white—if not strictly Anglo-Saxon—faces reflect the anxieties of jobless men, and, like western pioneers or Ellis Island immigrants, their hopes are fixed on a future very different from their past. Conscious role-players or not, in their departure to the woods these city boys are about to redramatize and renew for the country a classic American experience. Though the CCC ideal—and reality—may have seemed at times "backward" and primitive to enrollees, few could quarrel with the rejuvenating contrast the experience offered to the "dirt and depravity" of the crowded city.[15]

The agency record shots, figures 67 and 68, show the results on a dustbowl farm of emergency cover crop planting undertaken by the CCC in cooperation with the Soil Conservation Service. In themselves, the images are not remarkable; side by side, however, they represent an extraordinary transformation, a regeneration all the more striking because it is brought about by scientific knowledge. Agricultural order and bounty in the "green republic" are not left to chance, the photographs tell us; nature herself stands to benefit from science and technology. According to these deadpan documents, the CCC offers more than a pastoral experience. It teaches as well successful application of the technology, efficiency, and scientific outlook long valued in national tradition.

Almost irresistibly, it would seem, and from the start, CCC photography wrote large, if in contemporary terms, "the heroic figure of the idealized frontier farmer armed with that supreme agricultural weapon, the sacred plow." Such imagery, originally symbolic of a triumphant white race, emerged despite the fact that the agency's operations responded to a complex, multiracial reality that contradicted on many levels the classic frontier myth.[16] In addition to camps for white "juniors" (as young enrollees were called), veterans, and "local experienced men," the CCC established seventy-two projects, administered by the Bureau of Indian Affairs, on thirty-three reservations and by 1940 operated some one hundred and fifty segregated camps for black youths and veterans in twenty-seven states.[17] For the Indians, some of whom "reportedly were so undernourished that they collapsed when first put to work," the prospects offered by the CCC seemed like "a new El Dorado," as a local newspaper suggested.[18] Administered by the Bureau of Indian Affairs rather than by the Army, the CCC reservation projects established few camps and allowed enrollees, most of whom were married, to work from their homes, a departure from standard procedures which certainly complicated the process of public representation (see fig. 69).[19]

Through a series of administrative decisions, the original antidiscrimination clause in the CCC enabling legislation was eroded into a system of quotas and special regulations for blacks. These constraints effectively prevented them from enrolling in numbers representative of either their proportion of the population or of the fact that blacks made up a disproportionate majority of the unemployed and impoverished. Like Indians, black enrollees remained in camps much longer than white enrollees; nevertheless, official policy forbade the use of black officers in most positions of authority.[20] A "blot on the record of the CCC," the discriminatory practices were cloaked in "official silence," so that even "the ten Annual Reports of the Director of the C.C.C. contain not one word about Negro enrollees."[21]

Since neither the current status and history of minorities nor the conventions available for their representation reflected creditably upon the renewed mythology of the pioneer army, blacks and Indians did not, as a rule, appear in publicity. Few photographs of Indian enrollees were made before 1940, and, "on checking up," an official wrote in that year, "I find we have less than a dozen CCC photos showing negro enrollees at work." Plans had been made, however, to "assign a photographer shortly to go to colored CCC camps to get several sets of Kodachrome lantern slides and also photos for black and white slides."[22] In May of 1940, Wilfred J. Mead, the first and only professional photographer hired full time by the CCC, was sent from Washington to photograph black CCC camps in Virginia, North Carolina, and neighboring states. As figures 70 through 76 show us, Mead did not fail to include the classic stereotypes.[23]

The immediate purpose for such photographs was for exhibition at the Afra-Merican Exposition of seventy-five years of black progress held in Chicago in September 1940.[24] Beyond this purpose, however, and behind the hiring of Mead, was a major reconceptualization and reorganization of CCC publicity and agency objectives. A questionnaire circulated to several agencies by Roy Stryker, director of the well-known photography program at the Farm Security Administration (FSA), had provoked CCC officials to the realization that their photography program "has only been partially successful." "Rather drab" and lacking "variety, spice and life," CCC files contained few news or feature photographs because failures of "imagination and ability" disqualified most photographs from functions more complex than record-keeping. Stryker impressed CCC officials because he knew how to work out and assign the photographic "shooting scripts" that led to the picture series or photo-essay format much featured in current photojournalism. In addition, as a memo pointed out, "He has picked his photographers from fields other than professional photographers, and has found them eminently successful. One is an artist . . . others are more sociologists than photographers in background."[25]

However, even as the agency sought out new techniques and points of view in hopes of enhancing its public appeal, the outbreak of war in Europe brought changes that eroded its identity and purpose. Job opportunities in booming war industries and a shortage of farm labor cut drastically into white enrollment.[26] As early as 1937, demands for military training in the Corps were commonplace, and inevitably the agency's original relief purposes came into question. By 1940, with a vigorous noncombatant defense training program established by Congressional amendment,[27] defense-related training had officially become "the major objective" of the Corps. In a last ditch attempt to attract enrollees and affirm the agency's social place and national value, publicity was generated to "dispel the notion so firmly rooted in [the public mind] that [the CCC] is merely a work relief organization."[28]

The agency responded internally to the crisis by instituting a perceptible "tightening up" of its somewhat haphazard organizational structure, procedures, and sense of audience, as if not only industrial training but also bureaucratic efficiency and professionalism might be sources of new power and appeal. Wilfred Mead, whose 4,000-odd photographs present a coherent imagery and a thorough coverage, was valued not for artistic or sociological talents, but rather for his technical expertise, his knowledge of "news value" in photographs, and for the extra time he spent on clerical tasks "in order to help us establish a working photographic file as soon as possible."[29] Though Mead only worked close to Washington during spring and summer of 1940 before being sent on several western tours, McKinney's Public Relations Division lost no time in developing a well-organized scheme to exploit his photographs in selection offices, where potential enrollees might see them. Beginning in June 1940, the Division sent the first of several carefully mounted and captioned sets of photographs to all fifty state supervisors of selection. The procedure was so carefully managed that even supervisors' responses were controlled by a request for appreciative replies to be sent to Washington.

"They are exceptionally plain and portray clearly phases of CCC life," ran one of these apt if wooden missives.[30] And indeed, Mead's often posed, carefully lit photographs stand in sharp contrast to the prevailing photojournalistic aesthetic, which preferred spontaneity and candor as an earnest of truthful and reliable recording (figs. 77–85). In their clarity and in the equivalent or greater picture space machines occupy in relation to men, the photographs are suggestive of blueprints or diagrams of industrial relations. Their schematic quality—and the actual diagram in figure 82—echo the bureaucratic hierarchies in which they originated and to which they respond. Mead's photographs seem to be striving to express a subtly different relation to power

than earlier CCC photography had done. Fulfilling, though in an unexpected arena, the technocratic thrust that had been present in the agency from the beginning—side by side with its agrarian nostalgia—these images draw on a less familiar, if more "modern," iconography. Figures 77 and 81 virtually eliminate the natural, and when nature does appear, as in figures 78, 79, and 80, it assumes a decidedly subservient position. In Figure 79 it is being drilled in preparation for dynamiting, in figure 78 crushed by earth movers, and in the somewhat less violent figure 80, measured in preparation for a roadway. The production of wealth and power, both material and spiritual, is here removed entirely from traditional, organic rhythms and relationships to an industrial order whose dynamic responds only to the voracious needs of the war economy. In the new order, enrollees are, appropriately, modern machine tenders, no longer rustic husbandmen. More "spice, life," and excitement is generated by two anonymous and hooded figures operating a welder in the much reproduced figure 81, than by the static work portrait of surveyor George Steen (fig. 80).

Despite vigorous publicity, new selection techniques, and authorization of increased black selection, "morale [was] at the last stage of fatalism" in 1941, as Mead himself observed. Enrollment declined at the precipitous rate of six thousand a month, for the Corps could not compete with the high wages and sense of purpose offered by wartime industries. Unable to justify its continuing existence to Congress, the CCC was abolished on July 1, 1942.[31]

The agency's wartime dissolution seems an ironic if inevitable resolution of its multiple and even contradictory purposes. Like other New Deal agencies, the CCC acted as a modernizing force which helped ease the nation's transition to more urban and suburban ways of life. For all their praise of natural surroundings, CCC enrollees, like more sophisticated observers, recognized and valued the modernizing aspects of their experiences. The Corps was a way for Indians to learn "to manage for themselves in a modern world," Indian writer Oliver La Farge pointed out. "As an Americanizing influence, the CCC is perhaps without equal," wrote an enrollee who perceived that it "[got] immigrants' sons away from the old world settlements in our big cities." Even the modernizing effects of war were welcomed, at least by Colonel C. L. McGee, who, in a virtual parody of William James's famous essay, informed enrollees in a dedication address that "It's great to get into war. It broadens you."[32]

Because of the CCC's founding ideals and the beauty, resonance, and power Americans associated with them, their breakdown and replacement was a complex process with far-reaching implications. Such multiplicity of meaning as the Corps represents takes time to recognize and absorb, and we are fortunate to have photography among our means to insight. The images before us, both individually and in their relations to one another, propose new opportunities for understanding our history. Revealing more today than their makers ever meant them to do, they help us grasp more consciously the forces that have shaped American culture.

# Notes

1. Luther C. Wandall, "A Negro in the CCC," *The Crisis* (August 1935), 244; John A. Salmond, *The Civilian Conservation Corps, 1933–1942: A New Deal Case Study* (Durham, N.C., 1967), 6, 4.

2. Salmond, *The Civilian Conservation Corps*, 121–29.

3. Salmond, *The Civilian Conservation Corps*, 106, 121–29.

4. Jno. D. Guthrie, In Charge, ECW Information, to Regional Foresters, February 25, 1937, Records of CCC Work, 1933–42, General Correspondence, Information, Records of the Forest Service, Record Group 95, National Archives (hereafter cited as RG 95, NA).

5. John A. Salmond, "The Civilian Conservation Corps and the Negro," *Journal of American History* 52 (January 1966), 75.

6. Salmond, *The Civilian Conservation Corps*, v.

7. George P. Rawick, "The New Deal and Youth: The Civilian Conservation Corps, the National Youth Administration, the American Youth Congress" (Unpublished Ph. D. dissertation, University of Wisconsin, 1957) 33–34.

8. Salmond, "The Civilian Conservation Corps and the Negro," 76.

9. Rawick, "The New Deal," 171.

10. Salmond, *The Civilian Conservation Corps*, 131. A contemporary novel about unemployed young men in the Depression is Jack Conroy's *The Disinherited* (New York, 1963; originally published 1933.)

11. Leo Marx, *The Machine in the Garden: Technology and the Pastoral Ideal in America* (New York, 1964), 6.

12. Henry Nash Smith, *Virgin Land: The American West as Symbol and Myth* (New York, 1957), 13, 138–64.

13. Guy D. McKinney to Jno. D. Guthrie, February 13, 1937, Records of CCC Work, 1933–42, General Correspondence, Information, Records of the Forest Service, RG 95, NA; Granville E. Dickey, memorandum to Guy D. McKinney, October 8, 1940, Division of Planning and Public Relations, General Correspondence, Records of the CCC, Record Group 35, National Archives (hereafter cited as RG 35, NA).

14. *Happy Days* (May 20, 1933), 6, General Records, Records of the CCC, RG 35, NA.

15. Salmond, *The Civilian Conservation Corps*, 107; Smith, *Virgin Land*, 142. See also Richard Hofstadter, *The Age of Reform* (New York, 1955), 34–35.

16. Smith, *Virgin Land*, 138.

17. Salmond, *The Civilian Conservation Corps*, 33–34; Guthrie, memorandum for Mr. Dana Parkinson, April 4, 1940, Records of CCC Work, 1933–42, Information–News Digest– Press Releases, CCC Information–Exhibits–1940, Records of the Forest Service, RG 95, NA.

18. Donald L. Parman, *The Navajos and the New Deal* (New Haven, 1976), 35, 33.

19. Salmond, *The Civilian Conservation Corps*, 33.

20. Salmond, "The Civilian Conservation Corps and the Negro," 82–86.

21. Rawick, "The New Deal," 161–62.

22. Guthrie, memorandum for Mr. Dana Parkinson. See note 17.

23. Guthrie, memorandum for Mr. G. T. Backus, May 10, 1940, Records of CCC Work, Information, Records of the Forest Service, RG 95, NA.

24. Guthrie, memorandum for Mr. Dana Parkinson. See note 17.

25. Guthrie, memorandum for Mr. G. D. McKinney, November 3, 1939, Records of CCC Work, 1933–42, Information, Press Releases–Questionnaires, CCC Information–Photographs–1939, Records of the Forest Service, RG 95, NA.

26. Salmond, *The Civilian Conservation Corps*, 196–97.

27. Salmond, *The Civilian Conservation Corps*, 193, 196–97.

28. U.S. Office of Education, Statement on Development of CCC Public Relations Program, March 25, 1941, Division of Planning and Public Relations, General Correspondence, Records of the CCC, RG 35, NA.

29. McKinney, memorandum to McEntee, August 20, 1940, Division of Planning and Public Relations, General Correspondence, Records of the CCC, RG 35, NA.

30. W. Frank Persons, memorandum to McKinney, September 24, 1940, Division of Planning and Public Relations, General Correspondence, Records of the CCC, RG 35, NA.

31. Wilfred J. Mead to McKinney, July 14, 1941, Division of Planning and Public Relations, General Correspondence, Records of the CCC, RG 35, NA; Salmond, *The Civilian Conservation Corps*, 210, 217.

32. Oliver La Farge, *As Long as the Grass Shall Grow* (New York, 1940), 121; the enrollee is quoted in Salmond, *The Civilian Conservation Corps*, 130; see William James, "The Moral Equivalent of War," in his *Memories and Studies* (New York, 1912). For a discussion of the FSA as a modernizing force, and of the agency's photography in relation to the social documentary tradition, see Maren Stange, *"Symbols of Ideal Life": Social Documentary Photography in America, 1890–1950* (New York, 1988).

62

*Wilfred J. Mead*

Work project. Husky enrollee wielding sledge hammer in cracking rocks for park retaining walls and gutter bases. [Another print carries a different caption: "The slogan of the Civilian Conservation Corps is 'We can take it!' Building strong bodies is a major CCC objective. More than half of the enrollees who entered CCC during the last year were seventeen years of age. Work, calisthenics, marching drill, good food, and medical care feature the CCC health program."]

63

[A photograph of a painting, "Spirit of 1938," by Harry L. Rossoll, a forester in the Southern Region of the U.S. Forest Service. Copy photograph in Record Group 95, Records of the Forest Service, CCC Work, 1933–42, Information, 1939.]

64

The harvest.

65

CCC enrollee in the act of
planting a tree. One of the
outstanding features of the
work being accomplished by
this organization throughout
the region. Spartanburg,
South Carolina. September
26, 1941.

[From *Happy Days* 1 (May 20, 1933), 6.]

Part of the crowd that jammed the Federal building at Boston to get their names on the list for jobs for President Roosevelt's "Army of Reforestation." More than 1000 men waiting patiently for clerks to hand them their blanks to fill out.

67

View of barns with the drifted sand in front of them. Sand up to 6 feet deep in places. Beadle County, South Dakota. September 17, 1935.

68

Emergency cover crop planting of cane and Sudan grass, listed on the contour in cooperation with the Soil Conservation Service, brought the first control of the area seen around these good farm buildings abandoned during the 1935 drought and dust storms. In that year, soil drifts up to six feet deep surrounded these barns. Record dry weather in 1936 retarded stabilization. These crops were seeded in 1937 and by early August when this picture was taken had provided this effective protection against further wind blowing, paving the way for permanent stabilization and possible re-occupation of the farm under proper soil and moisture-saving farming methods. Beadle County, South Dakota. August 11, 1937.

*Wilfred J. Mead*

Indian Division. Pumping water from ditch. James Ortiz, a member of a CCC ID crew constructing a pipeline on the Santa Clara Pueblo lands, is starting a pump which will drain the pipeline trench of excess water seeping into it from Santa Clara Creek. This Indian worker is assisting in the building of a water diversion project which will supply the Santa Clara Pueblo lands and also the lands of adjoining pueblos with water for irrigation and drinking purposes. Indians from surrounding pueblos have cooperated in helping to build this pipeline on the Santa Clara Pueblo lands. Santa Clara Indian Reservation, Santa Fe, New Mexico. December 2, 1940.

*Wilfred J. Mead*

Forest nursery. Enrollee placing seedling pines in planting
rack. Beltsville, Maryland.
May 1940.

*Wilfred J. Mead*

CCC Negro enrollees. Road
surfacing. Enrollee at control
of road surfacing roller. Beltsville, Maryland. May 1940.

*72*

*Wilfred J. Mead*

Work projects. Group of
Negro enrollees filling in a
gully on eroded farm land.
Yanceyville, North Carolina.
May 5, 1940.

73

*Wilfred J. Mead*

Work projects. Negro en-
rollee operating tractor which
pulls terracer. Yanceyville,
North Carolina. May 5, 1940.

74

*Wilfred J. Mead*

Camp life. A bit of harmony is offered to fellow camp members of the CCC enrollee quartette. Yanceyville, North Carolina. May 5, 1940.

75

*Wilfred J. Mead*

Camp life. An impromptu jam session in camp recreation hall. Yanceyville, North Carolina. May 5, 1940.

76

*Wilfred J. Mead*

National defense training. Auto mechanics class. Negro enrollees from Camp NP-1, Cabin John, are engaged in various activities of a national defense auto mechanics training class in the school near Rockville, Maryland. Cabin John, Maryland. February 8, 1942.

77

*Wilfred J. Mead*

Tractor disassembling. Group
of CCC enrollees with in-
structors disassembling tractors. Central Repair Shop.
Salem, Virginia. June 5, 1940.

*Wilfred J. Mead*

Heavy equipment operation. George Zirkovich of Pittsburgh, Pennsylvania, learned to operate a tractor during one six-month enrollment period in the Corps. He left the Corps September 30th to join the Army tank corps. Photo shows Zirkovich at the controls of a "cat" dragging a fresno (earth remover) on a grading job at Westmoreland State Park, Virginia, where he was a member of CCC Camp Sp-19. Shortly after he entered the Corps he became a truck driver and graduated from that to tractors. Westmoreland State Park, Virginia. [1940].

*Wilfred J. Mead*

Road construction. CCC enrollee operating pneumatic jack hammer in drilling holes for dynamite "shots." This enrollee becomes expert in drilling and eventually if he so desires is moved on to the powder crew after a preparatory period of instruction in the use of dynamite before actually handling the explosive. Salem, Virginia. July 28, 1940.

*Wilfred J. Mead*

Surveying. Enrollee George
Steen of Pittsburgh, Pennsylvania, sights through a transit
during operations in surveying and laying out a curve on
forest road in the George
Washington National Forest.
George is a member of the
champion surveying crew of
the George Washington
National Forest. Camp
Roosevelt, F-1. Edinburg,
Virginia. July 19, 1941.

81

Electric welding. CCC
enrollee Herman Snead of
Roanoke, Virginia, operating
an electric welder under the
supervision of instructor
George Kaylor. One of the
many skills learned by CCC
enrollees in the Central Repair
Shops of the CCC where repair of automotive equipment
used in the camps is done.
Central Repair Shops. Salem,
Virginia. June 6, 1940.

*82*

Shop class room. Twelve CCC enrollees receive instruction in mechanical theory from O. W. Shelor. James J. McEntee (left), Director of the Corps, looks on. These timeout periods are given at the discretion of the shop superintendent to further advance the mechanical knowledge of the CCC boys. Central Repair Shop. Salem, Virginia. June 5, 1940.

*Wilfred J. Mead*

Work projects. Enrollee telephone lineman fastening telephone wire to glass insulator atop a telephone pole in the George Washington National Forest, Virginia. Camp Roosevelt, F-1. Edinburg, Virginia. July 20, 1940.

Job training. Camp mechanic demonstrating welding with an acetylene torch to a group of interested enrollees. This is an interval set aside for special job training instruction during the course of a day's work. Camp mechanics also act as instructors in evening classes for enrollees. Camp Roosevelt, F-1. Edinburg, Virginia. July 19, 1940.

# Uncle Sam's News Reel

TITLE REGISTERED U. S. PATENT OFFICE

1—CCC Director James J. McEntee inspects a tractor to be reconditioned.

## THE ROLE OF THE CCC
## IN THE DEFENSE PROGRAM

As President Roosevelt recently pointed out, the Civilian Conservation Corps is in a position not only to conserve natural and human resources but also to participate in non-combatant defense work. Repairing motorized equipment is one phase of that training.

Photos—Civilian Conservation Corps

2—In shop class rooms, boys are first instructed in mechanical theory.

3—A CCC enrollee does a touch-up paint job as part of the repair service.

4—Boys become skilled in operating electric welders.

OCTOBER 18, 1940

Continued on third rotogravure page

[*Uncle Sam's News Reel* made extensive use of Wilfred J. Mead's photographs. From Division of Planning and Public Relations, General Correspondence, 1933–42, News Clippings, Records of the CCC, Record Group 35, National Archives.]

# Figures of the Future:

## Photography of the National Youth Administration

## Sally Stein

Of all the federal agencies of the New Deal, the Farm Security Administration (FSA) made the most extensive use of photography. In trying to document thirties America, the FSA covered the greatest ground—conceptually as well as geographically. But the resulting cumulative portrait of the country was far from complete. Roy Stryker, chief of the FSA photographic operations, admitted as much in December 1942. In a letter to Aubrey Williams, director of the National Youth Administration (NYA), Stryker began by announcing that his own bureau within the FSA had been "taken over lock, stock, and barrel by the Office of War Information" (OWI). Stryker did not seem to mind a change that greatly expanded his field of publicity operations: "We will probably continue to do the same type of photography we have done in the past, but with a lot better justification." With the heightened authority of a wartime propagandist, Stryker proceeded to explain why he was writing Williams: "There is a big demand abroad—South America, Europe, Asia, and Africa—for pictures of this country as it really is—the main streets, the homes, the people at work and at play, the long landscape pictures, etc." Having thus enumerated some of the pastoral themes for which the FSA photographic files were justly famous, Stryker singled out another type of picture that would serve equally well in wartime but that the FSA could not deliver adequately from its collection: "One of the very insistent demands is for pictures of American youth, their problems and what has been done about them, what they look like and what they wear." On this basis he requested a meeting with Williams to discuss transfer of NYA photographic material to the OWI collection.[1]

Though beyond the scope of this essay, it is certainly not hard to imagine how the right sort of pictures of young adults could be ideally suited for wartime promotion of the American Dream abroad. One need only glance at a representative sampling of NYA photographs to understand why Stryker was so eager to incorporate the agency's visual material when he was no longer expected to confine his documentary interests to agriculture alone (figs. 86–88).

Obviously city folk look quite different from rural people, but even the NYA photographs of young farm laborers have a different feel than the typical FSA studies. The Oklahoma girl picking potatoes in the fields of Kern County, California, looks weary from her stoop labor yet by no means dispirited (fig. 89). Few FSA portraits project so strong a sense of self-possession, which may explain why in this instance we are not tempted to think in terms of "migrant mother" or "salt of the earth" or any number of equally clichéd rural types. Or consider the night shot of an outdoor screening of the New Deal documentary film, *The River,* a photo which offers an unprecedented view of rural youth as consumers rather than objects of thirties culture (fig. 90).

In another portrait of a young man riding the rails (fig. 91), the head is turned aside, staring presumably off in the distance, but the stare is more defiant than vacant, the jaw firm rather than slack, and the caption tells a story of rebellion—more commonly associated with the

1950s than the 1930s—as well as hardship: "He said he quit high school after two years, hung around home for a couple of years, and then got work as general kitchen help in a hotel. He had just been fired from a job of this kind in Los Angeles when he had 'blown up' and 'told the cook off.' He carried a clean white shirt and was prepared to look for work when his money was completely gone. . . . He had $1.80."[2] In this instance, the photographer Rondal Partridge may have contributed a large measure of the bravado to the figure of the adventurous hobo, for Partridge was no older than his subject and had thus qualified for NYA support while producing a photographic series on California youth. With remarkable consistency, however, NYA photographs conveyed an image of 1930s youth unwilling, however impoverished, to wholly accommodate themselves to Depression conditions.

Indeed, judging from these photographs, youths of this era were highly susceptible to the glamorous fantasies which continued to be churned out by mass media even as production in most sectors of the economy stagnated. One is reminded of the success of Busby Berkeley, Shirley Temple, Astaire and Rogers, by a view of a NYA Texas community recreation center in which teacher and student work intently at a mirror perfecting tap dance routines (fig. 92). The fascination with flight and speed, both as values in themselves and as potential avenues of self-advancement, is deftly communicated in the photo of two drafting students in a makeshift studio lined with sketches of futuristic sports cars and, more hyperbolically, in the view of a lone student raptly handling a model air plane (figs. 93, 94). The radio is a recurrent fixture in NYA photographs that document groups of youth learning a variety of skills: as assemblers, repairmen, broadcast technicians, announcers, and actors (fig. 95). One photo even shows a couple of advanced technical students peering at a small but apparently animated picture of a young woman on a television receiving set they had constructed themselves (fig. 96).

There is some irony in Stryker's sudden interest in NYA images of youth that express if not unlimited possibilities then undepleted reserves of energy. Only a year and a half before he sought to appropriate the photographic files, Stryker had criticized a proposal that the NYA provide more young people with programs in photography so that they themselves might document

their activities and simultaneously be exposed to a new career possibility in mass media. Citing the limited market for documentary photographers, the FSA publicist advocated a less ambitious course of training: "Try to develop an attitude toward laboratory work, that it is an end not a means. God knows we need more well-trained laboratory people who are willing to go into the laboratory and make that their last job."[3]

Fortunately the NYA did not heed Stryker's advice, for the pictorial record, while certainly uneven in quality, would be far less rich without the many amateur documents by juvenile participants in this New Deal program. Stryker, too, had reason to be thankful that the NYA did not follow his cautious advice, as later he would work closely with one photographer, Harold Corsini, who acquired his basic photographic skills under the auspices of the NYA Photographic Workshop in New York City.[4] Nevertheless, Stryker's discouraging prognosis reflected the bleak situation faced by youth in this era.

With a surplus of experienced workers seeking jobs, thirties youth were the last to be hired. At the same time, Depression layoffs of adult workers pushed teens to leave school with the aim of contributing to their families' reduced incomes, despite the fact that their chances for gainful employment were better if they at least completed their secondary education. Thus increasing numbers of young people faced extended periods of idleness before they obtained their first jobs. By 1937 the Census Bureau estimated that the population between the ages of sixteen and twenty-four numbered over twenty-one million and amounted to more than one sixth of the nation. Of these, five million were enrolled in school, seven million were employed full-time, and another two million could claim part-time jobs. But the official figures hardly described the full extent of youthful unemployment; the four million reported as unemployed excluded three million females who were neither employed nor in school but classified loosely as homemakers or otherwise occupied. Many of these young women would have been actively seeking work had they felt they had any chance of finding it. Moreover, an exceptionally high number of young adults with jobs were making too little to leave their families and start households of their own. Yet even according to the conservative figures of the Census Bureau, youth accounted for one-third of the unemployment in the Depression.[5]

The common sight of aimless kids hanging around led to widespread talk of a "youth problem," notwithstanding the general failure of the economic system. Though not the first time youth were labeled a problem, the Great Depression certainly intensified middle-class fears of an emerging generation of antisocial delinquents or, more extreme, well-organized revolutionaries. Special programs designed for the young presumably would curb these threats and might even soften the blows of the Depression by removing a sizable portion of the jobless from the labor market.

At the start of his presidency, Franklin Roosevelt tackled the "youth problem" by establishing the Civilian Conservation Corps (CCC). The rugged conditions of isolated camps for jobless men under army rule precluded much criticism that liberals were coddling the young or courting them for votes. But these conditions also limited the number of men willing to join the CCC and failed altogether to meet the needs of young women. As the Depression continued, it became evident that a far broader sector of the youthful population needed to be discouraged through relief measures from immediately entering the job market. Thus in the summer of 1935, Roosevelt established by executive order the NYA to administer a diverse set of relief programs designed for youth of both sexes, in and out of school.

The NYA would last for eight years. During the first four the agency was part of the mammoth Works Progress Administration (WPA). WPA chief Harry Hopkins appointed his assistant Aubrey Williams to administer the youth programs, and Williams, a former social worker, continued as NYA director until the agency folded in 1943. The NYA administered four different kinds of programs for youth aged sixteen to twenty-five from families on relief: student aid whereby needy high school, college, and graduate students were assigned work-study jobs in exchange for modest stipends to continue their studies; employment for out-of-school youth on work projects; vocational assistance in the form of job training through work projects and, whenever possible, job placement in the private sector; and organized recreation.[6]

In the student aid program, schools distributed the stipends—amounting to $6 per month for high school students and $15 per month for college students—and administered the work-study programs. Though NYA funds aided only a fraction of all needy students, between 1935 and 1943 over one and a half million high school pupils and six hundred thousand college students were thus enabled to continue their studies. As historian William Leuchtenberg has noted, most of the resulting student jobs were routine clerical assignments, but in some cases administrators tried to match jobs with a student's particular field of interest.[7] Not surprisingly, NYA photographs of the school program gave disproportionate emphasis to these challenging assignments, such as a carefully composed photograph of a pair of students assembling skeletons for biology class exhibits (fig. 97), an activity, the caption reports, that "saves University $35 to $50 per model."

NYA recreational programs were as swiftly implemented as student aid, but their ultimate value was far more questionable (see figs. 88, 92). One memorandum in the NYA manuscript archive states explicitly that both boys and girls canvassed in Illinois were desperate for help in finding jobs but felt little need to be assisted in leisure activities.[8] This survey underscores the pitfalls of interpreting photographs out of context, especially the seemingly artless, documentary-style publicity of the New Deal. Scenes of "wholesome" (and usually sex-segregated) leisure activities were a mainstay of NYA photography, yet despite the frequent appearance of spontaneity these pictures probably appealed far more to concerned adults than to the adolescent population.

The two other NYA categories intended specifically for unemployed out-of-school youth—work projects, and job training and placement—took considerably longer to be established but ultimately served the greatest number of youth and commanded the greatest share of the NYA budget. Between 1935 and 1943, over 2.6 million jobless youth received monthly relief checks ranging from $18 to $26 while they worked on community-based projects or were enrolled in job-training centers supervised by skilled workers. Like the WPA adult work projects, the early NYA work programs were highly labor intensive and depended largely on the organizational skills and creative vision of local administrators. Construction was usually limited to working on local parks, playgrounds, and swimming pools. The most ambitious projects built their own NYA youth centers or refurbished abandoned structures to serve as job training sites. The majority were far more modest, and if many qualified only as "make work" relief programs, a considerable number made imaginative use of relatively unskilled adolescents. A photograph of two young children waiting for a NYA toy lending library to open for the day effectively illustrates one ingenious small-scale youth program which served existing community needs and could hardly be charged with competing against workers in the private sector (fig. 98).

At the outset, organized educators had charged the NYA with unfair encroachment upon a field that traditionally enjoyed independence from the federal government. NYA personnel early recognized that organized labor could make similar accusations regarding the agency's establishment of unofficial apprenticeship programs. Official publications and scripts for speeches repeatedly made the point that the training youth workers received was not sufficiently advanced to qualify as full-fledged apprenticeship in a given trade. Still, the agency in the early years tried to avoid conflicts with unions by developing a large portion of its job programs within the still unorganized field of government work, particularly clerical work.[9]

One document of this type of inter-agency clerical apprenticeship presents a richly detailed view of the New York office of the U. S. Naturalization Service before the advent of central air conditioning rendered fans, open windows, and a relaxed summer dress code obsolete as ways to beat the heat (fig. 99). A similar scene of NYA boys performing clerical tasks under the supervision of an older female worker incidentally records one of the new uses of documentary photography as mural-size publicity—enlarged here in combination with bar graphs to promote the Rural Electrification Administration's (REA) successful penetration of the rural population (fig. 100).

The NYA consistently demonstrated great flexibility in devising small programs for youth in conjunction with other governmental agencies, public and private schools, community organizations, and private industries (figs. 101, 102). The ability to improvise served the agency well. In the late 1930s when most other Depression relief programs were either killed outright or subject to severe funding cuts, Congress was voting hefty budget increases for the NYA. As a result the NYA easily survived the dismantling in 1939 of its parent agency, the WPA, and even lasted a year after the CCC was killed in 1942 by a wartime Congress that sought to economize by slashing the budgets of all nonessential government programs. It is somewhat ironic that the NYA proved more adaptable to wartime exigencies than the CCC, since the NYA was viewed originally as a progressive alternative to the highly regimented, paramilitary youth program.

Mobilization entailed a basic reordering of the New Deal agency's priorities. During 1935–36, the first year of operations, the NYA spent $39 million, of which $15 million went to out-of-school programs and $24 million for student aid. In the fiscal year 1941–42, Congress allocated $122 million, of which $98.5 million was spent on out-of-school defense training programs and $16.5 million on student aid. Not only had priorities been reversed but the absolute amount spent to promote schooling had declined by nearly one-third.[10]

With the wartime trend toward greater centralization and capitalization of youth training centers, views of small-scale operations gave way to shots of far bigger facilities in which the size or complexity of machinery was as much the focus as the process of acquiring new skills (fig. 103). The premium placed on the productive capacity of a youthful work crew superseded the earlier theme of communal self-sufficiency or, to use a phrase that enjoyed wide currency throughout the 1930s, "production for use"—whereby much of the food, uniforms, and furniture utilized by a given project was also produced by that project.[11] Most dramatically, the wartime photographs evidence the profound change in job training for women, who suddenly were represented as part of the prospective industrial work force.

Nominally, the status of young women had always been a preeminent concern of the agency. After all, the growing number of unemployed young women constituted one reason in the mid thirties for adding the NYA to the preexisting ranks of New Deal agencies. Consequently the NYA never practiced overt sexual discrimination. Unlike the WPA which admitted less than 20 per cent women to its rolls (and the WPA had relatively high quotas for women), the NYA tried to ensure that the numbers of male and female youth receiving assistance were practically equal. On the other hand, although young women experienced no particular difficulty in signing up for NYA programs, the programs they were enrolled in made no attempt to provide them with the same marketable skills offered to young men in the NYA. While NYA boys in the 1930s learned a number of basic machine operations to help them realize their aptitude for various kinds of industrial work, most NYA girls of the Depression era were strongly encouraged to pursue an extended course in home economics. The instruction was geared towards work inside the home, though some of the training—particularly machine sewing and food preparation—also prepared women for wage work in the textile and food service industries or as paid domestics. These sorts of jobs were traditionally filled by women and not coincidentally were some of the lowest paying jobs in the economy.[12]

For many reasons, the NYA pursued a policy that far from encouraging young women to be self-supporting promoted female dependency instead. The New Deal's main priority was recovery rather than a sweeping socioeconomic transformation. Historian Lois Scharf, surveying the various setbacks faced by women of all classes during the Depression, found a general pattern of reaction in the 1930s: "Attention centered on unemployed men. The debate over the 'new woman' of the previous decade, who combined work and family, was completely subsumed by anxiety over the 'forgotten man' who combined no work with a possibly demoralized and disintegrating family."[13] Another reason for adhering to traditional role models had immediate practical value for the youth agency. Assigning girls to tasks that resembled the work of domestic maintenance resolved who would produce most of the uniforms and prepare and serve most of the food consumed by NYA boys. Thus motivated by present bureaucratic needs as well as a vision of the future, the Depression-era NYA reinforced the prevailing sexual division of labor.

We should not assume however that young girls were predisposed to accept a self-sacrificing role. The first book on the NYA, published in 1938, tacitly conceded resistance to these policies when it noted that occupational segregation was "perhaps the most complicated and most discussed question that has faced the NYA in the out-of-school program."[14] One small survey conducted by Illinois NYA director Mary Anderson focused specifically on the job expectations of unemployed girls. Work in stores and offices ranked as first and second preferences. Factory work was listed as third. Next came nursing. The final occupation was the least realistic and suggested the influence of mass magazines: interior decoration. Anderson noted that two forms of available local work had been explicitly rejected, each for

good reason: work as domestics due to the substandard wages, and work in a local cannery because of the unsanitary conditions.[15]

Consistent with a policy that minimized the significance of female wage work, NYA photography made no attempt to expose the labor conditions in private homes, canneries, and other workplaces that young women found unsatisfactory. Nevertheless, the visual records are very revealing about the marked racial stratifications within the sex-segmented program. Just as the NYA shaped its general policy towards women in terms of prevailing options for female employment, it tried to steer women of color into jobs that white women usually refused to fill. The agency obviously assumed that young black women would have set their sights lower and therefore would more readily accept the prospect of domestic work. Among the dozens of pictures in the NYA files depicting instruction in the finer points of domestic service, only blacks—or in the Southwest region, Hispanics—figure in the role of the prospective maid (fig. 104). These photographs also register resistance, since none of the women cast in this position made any effort to conceal her lack of enthusiasm.[16]

The same typology governed the promotion of commercial kitchen work. Although it is probable that the greatest overall number assigned to work in project kitchens were unskilled white women, black women most often figured in the official representations of food service work (fig. 105). As a rule, young white women were depicted performing less odious tasks: staffing the toy lending library and other social service projects; acquiring both manual and machine sewing skills; and even practicing something akin to interior decoration in situations where it was called for, as in the photograph made at the Missouri Fruit Experiment Station where NYA girls were photographed indoors, removed from field work, displaying the harvest to best advantage (fig. 106).

In mid 1939, the NYA received special appropriations to begin teaching industrial skills directly related to defense work. For over a year, the new projects admitted only males until massive hirings by private industry along with a newly instituted Selective Service reduced the pool of available young men.[17] The exact date when NYA defense projects were opened up to women is not clear—certainly no fanfare heralded this policy shift—but a precisely dated NYA photograph by Harold Corsini indicates that the process of admitting women to industrial training courses was still very new at the end of 1940 (fig. 107).

Corsini had been making photographs in the NYA since 1938—first as a student, then as a supervisor in the New York Photography Workshop—so the stiff formality in his picture was not due to lack of experience. This initiation scene was simply too novel to permit instant adaptation of established pictorial conventions. Whereas most NYA training shots played up the active role of the trainee, here four women stand awkwardly in semi-circular formation to observe a demonstration of welding technique. One young woman actually handles the acetylene burner, but the angle of view foregrounds the dynamic role of the instructor, bending closest to the metal as he guides the movement of the torch. His authority is signified by a white shop coat which contrasts with the girls' partial uniform of aprons over street clothes. His experience is conveyed by the fact that though the females wear protective gloves, he works casually, almost carelessly, with his bare hands.

The picture would be utterly static if it consisted only of these opposed elements; if it were, in other words, no more than the sum of its parts. But while the picture stresses difference, it also may be read narratively as a lesson in the obliteration of difference. Scanning the circular formation from left to right produces a radical transformation of the female type: beginning with the observer at left who stands furthest from the machine operation and whose shapely form, long hair, and pearl necklace are especially prominent in her profile position, facing the instructor 180 degrees away, each female figure appears more like—in position, in posture, and even, coincidentally, in the hairline—the practiced male welder.

Quite understandably, this androgynous motif never became a prototype for NYA photographs depicting women entering the field of defense work. The most effective wartime publicity would avoid unstable configurations that implied any radical subversion of traditional gender roles and power relationships. A quickly snapped sidewalk shot of NYA youth in formation for a New York mobilization parade is exceptional as it includes male and female welders congregating together (fig. 108). As a rule, NYA photographs pictured the female trainee comfortably settled in an industrial environment, already familiar with specific machine operations. Just as

Norman Rockwell's popular cover graphic celebrated the figure of "Rosie the Riveter" by downplaying all traces of male authority figures,[18] so too NYA imagery on the same theme usually framed men out of the picture to forestall a host of unsettling questions—questions on the one hand about the woman worker's sexuality, and on the other hand about her real skill level and employment future in this field of work (fig. 109).

The NYA's impact on wartime women workers merits far more study. Until now, research on the thousands of "Rosie the Riveters" has overlooked the initial process by which women made their way into heavy industries.[19] NYA photographs suggest one logical route, with the government assuming the costs for recruitment and rudimentary training of women. Furthermore, since NYA wartime publicity material continued to enshrine the ideology of domesticity, the agency's promotional operations may have been designed to prepare women to expect immediate demobilization from industrial work as soon as the war was over.

Certainly photographs from a 1941 NYA fashion show manifest a Janus-faced policy toward young women debating what they should do (and wear) as the Depression receded (figs. 110, 111). Two project outfits created by the Illinois NYA design department are worlds apart, as are the models' gestures and even their relationships to the viewer. Not only is the model in the revamped coverall framed to appear larger, but her gaze directed up and away from the photographer adds to the imposing effect. By contrast, the model in a pinafore and high heels turns her attention from the task at hand to smile directly at the viewer. Any bias created by the incontestable self-possession of the female welder is carefully redressed by the captions. The welding jumpsuit is described in strictly functional terms—"Fitted wrists and ankles permit wear of safety gloves and shoes"—whereas the dress is recommended for its ubiquitous charm: "Designed for wear by NYA cafeteria workers, the outfit is smart enough for general home use."

The specific political objectives behind most NYA images can only be inferred, for the evidence is limited. The national publicity office issued few written directives concerning the making or use of photographs, and little is known about either of the two main NYA staff photographers, Barbara H. Wright and Dan B. Nichols, though Wright at least committed to paper some general thoughts on NYA photography in 1941. Significantly, Wright's memo is found in the files of FSA publicist Roy Stryker, from whom she sometimes sought advice, and her memo began with first principles very close to Stryker's own. To be effective, NYA photography had to privilege the individual subject, "the youth himself," rather than an administrative perspective. But Wright also had adapted this central documentary tenet to a less comprehensive working method, narrowly focused on the experiences of youth inside NYA programs. To make the programs more appealing, she outlined scenes that would answer the common questions adolescents had about the character of youth centers: the quality of food and hygiene; the respect accorded to personal possessions and self-expression; and the chance to acquire consumer goods with NYA wages. Moreover, such images needed to have a spontaneous look if they were to be persuasive. Wright's own words were vivid on this score: "*Try to get away from posed shots.* They look dull, limp and without punch."[20] The memo leaves little doubt that the graphic vitality of the NYA picture collection was cultivated quite consciously, but it articulates motives for only the most basic (and fairly self-evident) NYA themes.

In just one area of NYA publicity were ideological motives clearly spelled out. The participation of black youth in the NYA occasioned an extended debate that addressed some of the racial implications of official imagery. The catalyst for this wide-ranging policy review was the prominent black educator Mary McLeod Bethune, who joined the initial NYA advisory committee in 1935 and quickly assumed a leadership position as head of the NYA Division of Negro Affairs. With the support of NYA director Aubrey Williams, an exceptionally progressive southerner, Bethune effected changes that would distinguish the youth agency from all other relief programs. This is not to suggest that black youth in the NYA could expect equal opportunity—the pictures of female service jobs evidence a clear system of racial tracking—but the concept of equal opportunity at least began to be articulated and it had measurable impact on some of the agency's operations.[21]

If only by providing minorities with a proportionate amount of relief, the NYA proved itself exceptional among New Deal agencies. Furthermore, youth projects mainly serving blacks were usually run by black professionals. In the area of higher education, the NYA sought

to reform rather than maintain the status quo; since money was allocated to schools within each state and many schools admitted no black students, Bethune succeeded in establishing a special fund (representing 5 percent of the total allotment to graduate students) for direct assistance to black college graduates pursuing professional training.[22]

This level of economic support for young black Americans was so unprecedented that it required special publicity. The Division of Negro Affairs produced its own material, including one of the more graphically sophisticated New Deal brochures, *The Tenth Youth*, as well as a short documentary film on NYA students at Wilberforce University. Not content with isolated pieces of publicity, by the late 1930s Bethune had created the new position of Negro Press Liaison, responsible for constantly gathering and disseminating news of NYA activities especially pertinent to blacks (fig. 112).[23]

Delivering services and keeping the black community informed of these services was Bethune's immediate objective, but no less important was her vision of a racially integrated New Deal. This vision was by no means realized in the 1930s. A substantive challenge to long-standing patterns of racial discrimination required the support of the federal government, yet the Roosevelt administration was unwilling to initiate legislation that would alienate the very powerful southern white faction of the Democratic party.[24] While major battles for civil rights were thereby postponed until after World War II, Bethune helped prepare the ground by waging psychological war against the mentality that buttressed the institutions of white supremacy.

Publicity is always a tricky business, especially for those without power. To offset the general invisibility of black Americans, Bethune courted publicity but worked skillfully to shape it as well. She traveled widely in her capacity as a New Deal representative, monitoring the progress of youth projects throughout the nation and capitalizing on these visits to educate local communities and NYA administrators of the potential possessed by black youth given the same training and treatment as whites. Racial incidents occurring in the course of her travels became opportunities to make similar points to mainstream America. On numerous occasions she publicly corrected white colleagues who referred to her as "Mary" rather than by her full name, Mrs. Mary McLeod Bethune, thus asserting that formality between races was preferable to a gratuitous assumption of familiarity.[25]

Bethune was just as sensitive to the sociological nuances of photographic communication and deliberately used the medium to put forth a new image of race relations. In numerous photos taken on Bethune's tours of regional NYA centers, her stately figure commands center stage, flanked by local administrators serving as guides. So far this conformed to the standard shot of a visiting dignitary, but added to this group pose were often at least two NYA participants—one black and one white (fig. 113). Even when the figure of Bethune was absent from the scene, most of the NYA interracial images seem too patently orchestrated to qualify as documentary records of ordinary scenes from everday life (figs. 114, 115). Faced with a choice between a naturalistic representation of the satus quo or an idealized image of harmonious race relations, Bethune's office must have decided that naturalism was a luxury that could not yet be afforded. Still there are a few NYA photographs including both black and white faces which seem more documentary than didactic (figs. 116, 117). A notable example is a boisterous scene of female welding apprentices congregating outside a Detroit training shop. The shot is simply too animated and the composition too lopsided to have been staged as evidence of wartime integration. Yet unlike the more common emblematic pairings photographed close-up, this is hardly a picture of racial balance, consisting as it does of a single black girl looking not completely comfortable in an otherwise all white crowd.

If now these symbolic maneuvers seem tame—and the gains made by such labored steps token at best—they were highly provocative at the time. The transcript of a June 1941 NYA conference provides excellent evidence of the charged political atmosphere, though that month was unusually tense as A. Phillip Randolph's growing March on Washington Movement made headlines with its plans to protest discrimination in wartime industry and the military.[26] In this context, a conference of NYA officials was briefed specifically on the proper handling of the Negro press—the representation of race relations having become a crucial symbolic weapon for those interested in maintaining the old order as well as those seeking to make way for the new.

Thus for the space of one morning, a black public-

ity specialist—identified in the transcript only by his last name, Browning—outlined a protocol that left little to chance or individual discretion. He began with first principles, noting that like the labor press black papers appreciated facts directly relevant to their constituency, "*how many Negroes* have been assigned on the NYA program; not just how many youth in all are on the program." Anticipating the way his white listeners might construe his remarks to perpetuate a racist double standard, he quickly advised against using the term "Negro Activities," adding this reminder: "We operate on the theory that we have an integrated program."

Translating these guidelines into visual terms, he warned that the usual pictures, "with Negroes just in the background . . . sent out for the state press will not do for the Negro press." This concrete reference to the dominant pictorial codes elicited defensive responses. The following hypothetical case was presented for his approval: "If we have a Negro youth in the background and a white youth in the foreground, it's all right if we don't have the Negro youth too far in the background? For the general press?" Browning assented though he clearly had in mind something more substantive than merely closing the pictorial gap between foreground and background. Just before this exchange, he had mentioned in passing what must have been emerging as the main publicity objective of the Division of Negro Affairs: "By carrying pictures of Negrows[sic] working next to white[sic], we can sell the idea to employers that if he[sic] puts them together he will not necessarily have a race riot."

While the assembled public relations men exhibited little courage in this dialogue, the transcript also underscores their limited powers to effect change. Publicity alone could not rectify the discrimination faced by blacks both in NYA training programs and in the work available to youth after training. For example, in Baltimore by 1941 white males had all been moved onto aviation projects leaving only blacks in the old NYA program—a situation that one of the PR men noted dryly was going to be "hard to sell to the general press."[27]

On the other hand, the use of photography for publicity also documents that the actual operations of NYA programs were sometimes more advanced than the official imagery prepared to represent them. In at least one instance, NYA photography accidentally recorded a normally functioning, integrated wartime work place, yet the agency's publicity apparatus suppressed this evidence rather than broadcasting it as a sign of social progress.

In early February 1942, an editor for the syndicated weekly Sunday news magazine *Parade* expressed interest in obtaining NYA material illustrating a young woman's entry into defense work after undergoing industrial training. Director of Information Norman Kuhne quickly arranged with the Illinois Information Officer John Ryckman for photographs to be shot in that state. The original idea of shooting the story at a major corporation like Caterpillar proved impossible. As Ryckman reported on February 12 when submitting the material his office had gathered, none of the well-known Illinois industries had resorted as yet to using women for defense work, so that the final work scenes were located in a small subsidiary shop. Despite this more humble setting, Kuhne first thought the photography a "swell job" when he wrote acknowledging receipt of pictures on February 14. The same day, however, Kuhne sent back to Illinois from Washington a second, more urgent message qualifying his enthusiasm. Close inspection had revealed that one of the pictures included a black in an otherwise white work group, and the Director of Information wanted the scene altered:

*The picture was trimmed out to eliminate the Negro youth because of the serious difficulties which arise from the publication of inter-racial pictures, and also to bring Reba closer to the foreground. Will you please print an 8 x 10, using this portion of the negative and send it air mail special. . . . In the event Parade asks for the negatives, be sure that on this particular one only this portion of the negative is sent. I assume this can be done either by cutting out a section of the negative or by etching out the other portions.*

It was censorship in a rush. Kuhne, anxious to meet the magazine's production schedule, simultaneously mailed to *Parade* all but the interracial scene along with a quickly concocted explanation for the missing picture which he promised would soon complete the set:

*The 28th picture, which is subcaptioned No. 11 in the series, will be sent to you in a day to two as soon as a new print is made. These prints were batted off in a rush . . . and a few of them don't have the quality that a more careful printing job would produce. However, this will give you a pretty good idea of the yarn, which I think is a very exciting one, and if you want the negatives for making some new*

*prints according to your own specifications we will be very glad to loan them to you.*[28]

A one-page photo essay titled "Women Make Tools of War" appeared in the 29 March 1942 issue of *Parade* (fig. 118). Of the twenty-eight pictures submitted, eight had been selected and sequenced to illustrate the recent changes in the life of one Reba Connert, initially employed as a stenographer in a dry cleaning establishment, next enrolled in the NYA to gain familiarity with some basic industrial machinery, followed by scenes of her in line to punch a factory timeclock and running a metal shaping machine on her own.

From the published story there is no way of knowing whether any of the work place pictures selected derived from the critical exposure in the original set, and unfortunately the National Archives does not contain either negatives or prints from this assignment. How the magazine editors would have treated the image had they seen it before the black figure had been cut from the scene is a moot question. Even had the editors chosen to run the picture, it probably would not have made much difference, especially if it were an isolated instance. Nevertheless, the previously formulated strategy of the Division of Negro Affairs—promoting pictures of blacks working alongside whites to encourage color blind hiring practices—had an opportunity to be tested, and it was an opportunity consciously rejected as more trouble than it was worth.

Thus the published "yarn" presented defense work in very familiar terms. Black workers remained outside the wartime picture. Furthermore, though this particular narrative of Rosie the Riveter began as a tale of work advancement, it ended in the manner of a traditional romance—with a closing shot away from work, at the local coffee shop, with a caption structured to undercut the female character's importance other than as a soldier's date: "ON HER DAY OFF Reba usually goes out with her boy friend, Corporal George Johnson, U. S. Army."[29]

What explains the agency's about-face from a progressive to a conservative position on the issue of race? The key figure in this episode, Kuhne, had just been appointed Director of Information. He probably wanted to avoid controversy in the first months of his job, especially when the NYA faced grave cutbacks as a nonessential wartime agency. Having recently been assigned to answer the charges levelled by Southern conservative politicans seeking to cut all funding for NYA photographic operations, Kuhne was keenly aware how vulnerable the youth agency was.[30] Though the Director of Information surely recognized that budgetary attacks were largely a pretext for unstated hostility to the NYA's progressive activities, so too he must have realized that national publicity amounting to the agency's endorsement of integrated work places would only fuel the campaign to abolish the NYA.

There was probably another reason why Kuhne was so ready to tone down the agency's commitment to social change. A story in a syndicated weekly like *Parade* was a coup for any government publicist, but it was an extraordinary break for the NYA. Up to that time, the NYA had little success obtaining space in national media. My research has uncovered only one NYA photo previously published in a major magazine while numerous internal memos attest to failed efforts to place publicity.[31] Given this poor track record, Kuhne might well have figured that a lily-white image would have a better reception with the mainstream media.

But if that serves to answer one question, it opens up another. Why, given the quality of NYA photography, was the agency unable to channel the material into mainstream outlets following the lead of Stryker's FSA publicity outfit? For one reason, the FSA had an advantage in terms of subject matter. The displaced farmer was *the* resonant image of the Great Depression. At the very end of the era, writer James Agee noted acidly that the figure of the sharecropper had been made the subject of widespread symbolic as well as economic exploitation.[32]

While youth were also a cause for concern, the typical media treatment of youth departed dramatically from the way the NYA represented them. For example, in a special *Life* magazine issue devoted to the "youth problem," college students at the Maryland Institute, Vassar, Sarah Lawrence, Princeton, and Berkeley predominated. Only a couple of stories profiled working-class youth, though the CCC rated a two-page spread alternately stressing well-defined muscles and well-ordered camps, accompanied by a short text cheerfully noting the resemblance between the CCC and the fascist youth movements.[33]

Such a survey had no use for NYA youth who fit neither a carefree nor highly regimented image. Close-ups of NYA youth would show them to be all too ragged, despite the obvious attempts to maintain a sense of style and individuality; likewise group pictures tended to emphasize a somewhat anarchic camaraderie rather than *esprit de corps*. Thus while the agency actively sought outside coverage, it usually found itself at odds with the media's romantic vision of youth. One agency memo summarizes the failed courtship of Hollywood and the NYA: "A couple of gals who write for Universal . . . were all steamed up about the current interest in youth from the girl angle. They outlined a plot . . . which did prominently feature the NYA, but their representation was about 100% inaccurate . . . a sort of Bohemian rendezvous for beautiful young gals who spent most of their time prancing around in fancy clothes, playing with the boys and generally raising hell like girls at college." When Universal was informed that the agency could never approve such a departure from prosaic reality, "the two girls from Universal immediately lost interest in the NYA and began to try to think of some other locale for their youth story."[34]

Yet the publicity problem was not confined to the subject matter or the terms of representation. The problem was compounded by the way the agency organized its own publicity resources. Indeed the contrast between the structure of the NYA photographic operation and that of the FSA sheds light on what may have been Stryker's most effective contribution to FSA publicity: an efficiently organized archive designed to maximize the circulation of photos in a wide set of contexts.[35]

Overall the NYA relied more upon local initiative than the FSA, though even the FSA programs varied from state to state according to the discretion of local advisory boards and administrators. While publicity work in the NYA was correspondingly dispersed, FSA publicity as shaped by Stryker was highly centralized. When Stryker first began work as an Information Specialist for the Resettlement Administration (RA) in 1935, the agency's photographic documentation was regionally produced. Results varied depending upon talent and the availability of adequate equipment. From Stryker's perspective, the system invited amateurish dabbling and a surplus of prosaic project records. He quickly set about calling in all professional cameras on loan from Washington and informed the regional offices that from now on they would have to budget for any photographic supplies they used on their own initiative. In the process of instituting these new policies, he minced no words pronouncing most of the local pictures worthless, thereby establishing his national office as the seat of judgment in all publicity matters.

Of course this reorganization provoked resistance. Regional administrators protested the hub system's inability to meet their local needs. Even when scheduling problems were surmounted, pictures emanating from Washington represented an alien conception—genre scenes, rather than specific documentation for local news stories. Letters criticizing both the style and scale of the standard 8 x 10s produced by Stryker's office consistently implied that Stryker had lost touch with small town publicity operations: "98 percent of our requirements call for nothing more expensive than a good, sharp, glossy print not larger than 3″ by 6″. . . . Newspapers are inclined to ignore artistic value. . . . The subject matter must be to the point and illustrate some particular point."[36]

Stryker, who maintained a homespun style, must have bristled at the charge of being too arty. Nevertheless, though he made greater effort as time went on to handle regional requests diplomatically, he adhered strictly to his concept of a central archive comprised of photographs illustrating *general* social problems. The notable success Stryker enjoyed publicizing rural conditions in national media only made him more dismissive of alternative methods. When called upon to review the results of a 1940 inter-agency publicity survey, Stryker ignored data indicating a preference for newspaper over magazine coverage, contending instead that "all agencies want more than anything else dramatic picture coverage of their programs which is as widely usable as possible and not limited by a date-line."[37]

NYA officials did not condemn dramatic picture coverage but no one inside the agency was willing to take the necessary steps to make feature stories the top priority. Professionalization of picture-taking would have run counter to the agency's commitment to providing youth with a wide variety of educational opportunities. Centralization of resources would also have risked alienating local institutions co-sponsoring NYA programs, as they stood to gain more publicity from "spot" news and regional exhibits than from stories with a broader scope for national media.

On the other hand, Stryker's media success was too impressive to be wholly ignored. Accordingly, the youth agency attempted to maintain its decentralized photo operations *and also* build up a modest photography outfit based in Washington and clearly styled upon Stryker's FSA model. In early 1939 the NYA chose for its first staff photographer Barbara Wright whom Stryker already knew and probably recommended for the job. At the same time, the NYA began to contract out for standardized prints from FSA and to copy FSA procedures for storing photographs with the idea of collecting and cataloguing copies of images produced at the grass-roots level.[38]

But these half-measures toward creating a permanent, media-oriented archive yielded limited practical results. The Washington office lacked staff to organize and maintain a photographic file or open it to the public.[39] The various states' output of pictures continued to remain elusive as well as uncoordinated. And a single national photographer—or even two photographers during the peak mobilization period—would be forever pinch-hitting for all those regions lacking any documentation, thus unable to produce the kind of in-depth coverage suitable for feature stories. With limited funds for photography, the agency's dual focus did not greatly further either national or regional publicity operations.

To measure the success or failure of local NYA publicity efforts would necessitate a detailed study of newspaper coverage of youth in various regions. It is clear from the national records, however, that many state offices were hard-pressed to support more than a primitive photographic program. In the summer of 1941, staff photographer Barbara Wright was temporarily transferred to the Denver office to help develop photographic programs in the Western region. Her reports back to Washington describe an enthusiastic atmosphere but no collection of records of past activities and abysmal conditions for any sort of publishable photography. On arrival in Colorado, Wright discovered that her standard press camera used a negative too large for the amateur enlargers rigged up in the NYA darkroom. In order to process her work for local use, she travelled to a New Mexico NYA center only to face an equally poor setup: "They have an old piece of bottle or something for an enlarging lens. . . . The supervisor is a fine craftsmen [sic] but can't help but make the blowups look like

Kodak-as-you-go-snapshots under very-deep water." In desperation, Wright requested that Washington dispatch pictures to promote western activities, knowing how thin the national files were for each area; indeed, as soon as she had returned to Washington she would be requesting the Denver office to send her the negatives she recently had shot there, "as we could release them right away."[40]

Obviously, the decentralized system left the national office just as hamstrung as the individual state offices. The previously discussed *Parade* story is an illustration of bureaucratic censorship, but it also illustrates the general difficulties of orchestrating any publicity job by an attenuated long-distance process. When the same information director Norman Kuhne tried to prepare a pictorial report on NYA defense training in early 1942, he shelved the idea after failing to secure the cooperation of state offices that balked at the prospect of loaning Washington their best negatives.[41]

As the major source of NYA photographs were young amateurs in the youth program, development of a central collection was especially problematic. Unless a workshop supervisor specifically requested a copy of a picture for record or publicity purposes, photography students felt free to take home the best examples of their work. As a result, even those state programs like New York with large, active photography programs are represented in the national file by a small set of pictures which focus primarily on youth in defense activities. In contrast to the Washington FSA offices which were widely known as an accessible source of diverse documentary images, the NYA national offices never succeeded in amassing the stockpile of pictures that would attract the interest of publishers in the private sector. When the NYA was liquidated in 1943, around the same time that Stryker's photographic operation was transferred from the FSA to the OWI, the Washington print files of the NYA amounted to approximately six thousand photographs—many of which lacked original negatives or even minimal caption information—as compared with the efficiently organized FSA archive of nearly seventy thousand catalogued images.[42]

One group of photographs in the NYA collection suggests an alternative way the agency might have expanded its collection of visual material without following the bureaucratic course charted by the FSA. The previously discussed portraits of a young female farmworker (fig. 89) and an unemployed boy riding the rails (fig. 91) were part of a larger, loosely structured document of California youth, produced in the spring of 1940 by Rondal Partridge, who received in exchange a temporary youth stipend. The resulting series described adolescence with both passion and a thorough attention to material circumstances. Careful captions provided very useful background information, but Partridge's pictures made no specious claims to objectivity. An older professional probably would have resisted the temptation to frame a group of marching ROTC students with a street sign directing traffic, "KEEP TO RIGHT" (fig. 119). Partridge's pacifist sympathies clearly informed his documentation of student protests on the UC Berkeley campus, and of the Navy's recruitment of kids who had discovered no more viable options than enlistment (figs. 120, 121).[43] The photographer was fascinated with various adolescent subcultures surfacing in this era: a small band of motorcyclists, with girlfriends in tow, shot from below and behind (fig. 122); an audience crowding a swing band, shot from above to include only the musicians' feet and sheet music, thus stressing the rhythm and order as well as the sheer energy of the entertainment (fig. 123). His most poignant pictures are the tense scenes of applicants waiting to be interviewed for wartime jobs at Lockheed, recent demand for semi-skilled production workers having raised salaries from $.90 to $1.02 an hour (fig. 124).[44] These details and others noted just as sharply began to provide a more varied picture of the prospects faced by youth as the decade-long Depression continued into the 1940s, even as the war was in sight (figs. 125–127).

There is no record of official reaction to the group of two hundred photographs Partridge submitted. Officials may have found these views so subjective as to defy any bureaucratic use. In any case, no special effort was made to exhibit or publish this series, or to encourage either Partridge or other youth to continue photographing in this open-ended fashion.

The failure to explore the possibility of NYA participants becoming full-fledged producers of documentary essays indicates the limits of the agency's use of both the photographic medium and its young constituency. It is true that Partridge's photography was too exceptional to serve as a standard for other juvenile work. He had not only a basic talent for photography but a precocious amount of experience, as well as special access to equipment. The son of the well-known California photographer Imogen Cunningham, by his late teens Partridge had already worked as an assistant to the great documentary photographer Dorothea Lange.[45]

Nevertheless, other young photographers in the NYA made strong enough pictures to suggest that they were capable of undertaking similar assignments (figs. 128–130). Certainly their training would have been more challenging had they been expected to contribute extended visual commentaries focusing on specific themes. Certainly, too, the historical record would contain richer material on what it was like to come of age during the New Deal if a diverse group of working-class youth—male and female, white and black, urban and rural—had been seriously encouraged to use photography to describe their perceptions of a society in crisis.

# Notes

1. Roy Stryker to Aubrey Williams, December 1, 1942, in textual records of the FSA, Historical Section, Box 5, Lot 12024, Division of Prints and Photographs, Library of Congress (hereafter cited as P&P, LC). For reasons not detailed in either the FSA or NYA records, the wholesale transfer of NYA photography sought by Stryker never took place. Instead, a small group of copy prints and negatives from the NYA collection of photographs was incorporated into the massive picture file of the Office of War Information, now filed in P&P, LC.

2. Original caption to Partridge photograph no. 13, in California sub-group, Record Group 119–NYA–Cal. All subsequent quotes from captions to NYA photographs are from the original mount boards of the file photographs (or labels attached to the backs of unmounted photos) in Record Group 119 of the Still Picture Branch of the National Archives (hereafter cited as RG 119, NA).

3. Stryker to Barbara Wright, August 12, 1941, Box 4, Lot 12024, P&P, LC.

4. Steven W. Plattner, *Roy Stryker, U.S.A., 1943–1950* (Austin, 1983), 37.

5. Census figures cited in Betty and Ernest K. Lindley, *A New Deal for Youth* (New York, 1938), 6.

6. The most extensive discussion of the NYA's programs and politics—including the initially harmonious and subsequently fractious relationship between communist youth groups and the federal youth program—is provided in the second half of George Philip Rawick's comparative study of the CCC and NYA, *The New Deal and Youth* (Ann Arbor, University Microfilm, 1957), 171–393. On the progressive leadership of the director of the NYA, see John A. Salmond's recent biography of Aubrey Williams, *A Southern Rebel* (Chapel Hill, 1983), 120–50.

7. *Final Report of the National Youth Administration* (Washington, 1944), 58; William Leuchtenburg, *Franklin D. Roosevelt and the New Deal* (New York, 1963), 129.

8. "Special Report: 'Find-A-Job Club,' Belvidere, Ill.," (n.p.), submitted by Illinois NYA Director, Mary Anderson, n.d. (ca. June, 1939) in NYA files, "Info. Service, Director Herb Little, Old Corresp. G–L," RG 119, NA.

9. *Final Report,* 104–7, 163.

10. Statistics in a memo by Norman Kuhne, Director of Information, dated March 4, 1942, in NYA files, "Info. Service, Current Files, Misc.," RG 119, NA.

11. On the wartime excision of "production for use" rhetoric, compare handwritten and subsequent revised typescript of story prepared for official release by photographer Barbara Wright, "NYA's contribution to the shipbuilding Program for the United Nations at War," dated January 1942, in NYA files, "Info. Service, Current Files, Info. Personnel, A to L," RG

119, NA. (Though the first draft is annotated, "Barbara Wright's Trade Magazine Story," I found no evidence that the story ever ran.)

12. *Final Report,* 12–13; Lois Scharf, *To Work and To Wed* (Westport, 1980), 123.

13. Scharf, *To Work and To Wed,* 137; on the generally conservative tenor of New Deal policy, see Barton J. Bernstein, "The New Deal: The Conservative Achievement of Liberal Reform," in Bernstein, ed., *Towards a New Past: Dissenting Essays in American History* (New York, 1968), 263–88.

14. Lindley, *A New Deal for Youth,* 52–53.

15. See note 8 above.

16. The NYA *Final Report* frankly acknowledged the failure of all of its domestic training programs. See 168–69.

17. *Final Report,* 151–52.

18. See Norman Rockwell's cover for *The Saturday Evening Post,* May 29, 1943.

19. For a concise discussion of wartime women's employment in the auto industry which also notes other feminist scholarship in this field, see Ruth Milkman, "Redefining 'Women's Work': The Sexual Division of Labor in the Auto Industry During World War II," *Feminist Studies* 8 (Summer 1982), 337–72.

20. Letter from Barbara Wright to Stryker, July 12, 1941, with attached memo intended for distribution to regional NYA publicity offices, Box 4, Lot 12024, P&P, LC.

21. For a biography of Bethune, see Rackham Holt, *Mary McLeod Bethune* (Garden City, 1964). For conflicting assessments of the extent of Bethune's influence on New Deal policy in general, see the two pertinent essays in Bernard Sternsher, ed., *The Negro in Depression and War* (Chicago, 1969): Mary MacLeod Bethune, "My Secret Talks with FDR," 53–65, and Allan Morrison, "The Secret Papers of FDR," 66–77.

22. Rawick, *The New Deal and Youth,* 233.

23. Theodore Posten, hired in 1939 by Bethune to be first Negro Press Liaison in the NYA would by 1941 have transferred to the wartime Office of Production Management where he investigated race relations in heavy industry for Sidney Hillman's office, as noted in NYA files, "Info. Service, Old. Corresp., Misc.-Morris," RG 119, NA. *The Tenth Youth* was first published in 1938 and reprinted in 1940, as noted in Rawick, *The New Deal and Youth,* 402.

24. See George B. Tindall, *The Emergence of the New South: 1913–1945* (Baton Rouge, 1967), 555. Leuchtenberg offers a similar assessment, in *Franklin D. Roosevelt and the New Deal,* 185–86.

25. Holt, *Mary McLeod Bethune,* 239.

26. Richard M. Dalfiume, "The 'Forgotten Years' of the Negro Revolution," in Sternsher, ed., *The Negro in Depression and War,* 305–6.

27. June 21, 1941, meeting of regional administrators with Committee on Negro Affairs, "Info. and Public Relations Conference," xxx–xxxiv, in NYA files, "Info. Service, Old. Corr., G-L," RG 119, NA.

28. All correspondence I have cited relating to preparation of the *Parade* story is in NYA files, "Info. Service, Current files, N-R," RG 119, NA.

29. *Parade,* "Women Make Tools of War," March 29, 1942, 13.

30. See Kuhne to Williams, November 1, 1941, in NYA files "Info. Service, Current Files, Personnel, A-L, under 'K'," RG 119, NA.

31. The one picture in question was an ingenious shot of a boy seen through semi-transparent drafting tools. Since the photo was made by a member of the photography workshop at the NYA Quoddy, Maine, resident center, it was especially impressive in that it not only held its own but stood out when it appeared among a dozen professional images in a *Fortune* essay on the general topic of youth. See "Youth," *Fortune* (May 1940), 90, lower left image captioned "Quoddy Government Project Gives Hope." In this instance, however, the NYA gained little from the exposure. While *Fortune* credited all the professional photos used in the story, it ran no credit with this picture to indicate that it was not only of, but by, a NYA youth. A similar image, No. 119-S-15B-1, is filed in the Maine sub-group of the NYA picture collection, RG 119, NA. Photographer Harold Corsini confirmed that publication in mainstream media outlets was the elusive goal of NYA photography projects when he recently recalled the standard type of work produced in the NYA Photographic Workshop in New York City: "Most of our photography was shot in a sort of journalistic style . . . It was our constant hope to get one of our pictures in *Life* or *Look.* We never succeeded." Letter from Corsini to author, March 8, 1986.

32. James Agee, *Let Us Now Praise Famous Men* (Boston, 1941), 454–56.

33. "Germany, Italy, Russia and Japan each has its labor battalions which do much the same kind of work but there is nothing to match America's CCC outside the dictatorship countries." *Life,* June 6, 1938, 56.

34. Unsigned May 20, 1940, memo beginning "Dear Albert [Tewksbury, head of California NYA Information Office]" in NYA files, "Info. Service, Old Corr. E-F," RG 119, NA.

35. For a general theoretical critique of the bureaucratic motives and uses of the archive, see Allan Sekula's essay, "Photography between Labour and Capital," especially the introductory section, "Reading an Archive" in Benjamin H. D. Buchloh and Robert Wilkie, eds., *Mining Photographs and Other Pictures, 1948–1968* (Halifax, Nova Scotia, 1983), 193–268.

36. O. E. Jones, Information Advisor to the Little Rock Resettlement Office, to Stryker, date stamped October 25, 1935, p. 2. For similar arguments from other regional offices, see D. P. Trent to R. G. Tugwell, Stryker files, LC Box 2, date stamped September 15, 1936, and E. A. Starch to R. G.

Tugwell, date stamped October 16, 1936, Box 2, Lot 12024, P&P, LC.

37. Stryker memo dated January 31, 1940, with attached "Report on Answers to Federal Security Questionnaire," in "Stryker Project" file, Box 3, Paul Vanderbilt Papers, Archives of American Art, Smithsonian Institution.

38. See FSA internal office memo titled "Gossip Sheet" dated April 3, 1939, which includes on p. 2 this entry: "Barbara Wright now has a job with the National Youth Administration; . . . She seems to be getting along very well. We are doing all the laboratory work for this outfit." "Stryker Project" file, Box 3, Paul Vanderbilt Papers, Archives of American Art, Smithsonian Institution; likewise in Stryker office files a December 9, 1937, letter from Stryker to Mrs. E. Little of the *New York Times Magazine* recommending that the magazine editor consider for publication a photo essay Wright had just made in the South (Box 3, Lot 12024, P&P, LC). Unfortunately, this early work by Wright is not in the file, and Wright's career after the war is similarly hard to trace as she reportedly married and moved to England in the early 1950s. On the direct influence of FSA photography on the NYA's attempt to develop an archive, see March 8, 1939, memo from Karl Borders to G. S. Holmes, in NYA files "Info. Service, Borders, Library and Photographic Files," RG 119, NA.

39. On the limited operating capacity of the NYA archive in 1940, see the same Federal Security Questionnaire cited above in note 37.

40. Wright to Kuhne, August 12, 1941; and Wright to Amer Lehman, Colorado State Youth Administrator, November 14, 1941, in "State Files, Colorado, Office of Info.," RG 119, NA.

41. See Kuhne correspondence, especially January 24, 1942, to John Bryan, in NYA files, "Info. Services, Current Files, B," RG 119, NA; that the projected report never progressed beyond initial planning stages was confirmed by Arnold Eagle in a phone conversation, July 12, 1985.

42. From telephone conversations in July 1985 with NYA photography supervisors Arnold Eagle and Harold Corsini. On approximate volume of the NYA central picture file in 1943, see December 12, 1942, memo from Paul Vanderbilt to Roy Stryker reporting his survey of the NYA collection of photographs, Box 5, LC 12024, P&P, LC. NYA photographs in RG 119 currently number 20,900 according to the National Archives finding aid prepared by Mayfield S. Bray, "Still Pictures in the Audiovisual Archives Division of the National Archives," (Washington: National Archives, 1972), 27.; Vanderbilt possibly estimated low, but well over half of the present collection is comprised of various state archives which were absorbed in the Washington file only after the NYA folded in mid 1943. As for the exact size of the FSA collection of photographic prints in early 1943, no precise figures were kept for the number of prints on file in any given year so that seventy thousand is a round figure, possibly somewhat inflated, but confirmed as a reasonable estimate by LC archivists who in 1985–86 were preparing a computer index of the collection.

43. The personal appeal of the pacifist movement is just as apparent in the photographer's captions, particularly the general caption Partridge wrote to introduce his series on the UC Berkeley Student Peace Strike:

*According to the Daily Californian, an estimated million students in the United States participated in the 1940 annual April Peace Strike, although demonstrations were not held in London and Paris as they had been last year. At the University of California about 10% of the student body gathered outside of Sather Gate, the southern boundary of the campus, to hear students and speakers sponsored by the "Yanks Are Not Coming" committee: Revels Clayton, Negro CIO leader, Abbot Simon, secretary of the World Youth Congress, and the Reverend Don Chase, a Methodist minister. The demonstration was supported locally by several student political, religious, social and professional organizations. Nothing constructive was brought up by the speakers. There was no 'radicalism,' which is supposed to be characteristic of University of California Peace Meetings. At the University of California the peace meetings and compulsory ROTC have for several years been problems of paramount interest to certain active minorities in the student body. During the spring semester of this year, the A.S.U.C. [Associated Students of the University of California] Peace Committee made a study of the compulsory ROTC of which Oswald Garrison Villard said in his column in The Nation (March 23, 1940): 'It is by all odds the clearest and most convincing argument against compulsory military drill yet produced.' This study was first presented to the student body for a vote, which accepted it in a three-to-one ratio, and then submitted, with the vote, to the Regents at their March meeting. However, the effectiveness of this petition is best measured by the fact that regular ROTC classes were still in session during the peace strike. [All Partridge caption material is collected in a file labeled "119 CAL" in RG 119, NA.]*

44. The general caption to Partridge's series on job seekers at Lockheed's L. A. offices attempts a broad look at the dislocations that resulted with rapid mobilization of wartime industries:

*One of the phenomena of the aircraft employment in the early months of 1940, after the cash and carry program had been put into effect, was the crowds of men in the lines outside the personnel departments of the aircraft plants. A line of two thousand a day was not unusual. After a few months the lines were reduced to about a hundred a day, due to the exhaustion of most of the available local material and the closer cooperation between vocational schools and plants. Many of the persons in the lines at this time had appointments. About fifty to seventy-five percent of the applicants are young men in their late teens or early twenties. Many of them have had some aircraft experience in the Naval Reserve, the NYA aircraft shops or private industry. Others have had vocational training in sheet metal work or die and pattern work or have had experience as machinists. Many of them are here not because they need jobs but because they feel that working in an airplane factory is more romantic than pumping gas or whatever other job they may have. A recent general raise in wages in the skilled classifications from an hourly rate of $.90 to $1.02 is a more material inducement.*

The actual screening procedures and underlying objectives were described by Partridge in a separate caption to a small series on the typical testing program instituted by Lockheed in Oakland, California, as part of its regional expansion:

*Those with mechanical vocational training and able to guarantee a two year working period were confronted with the Rumm-Wadsworth Temperament test and the Otis Self-Administering tests of mental ability. The effect of this stringent examination was to sort out those best keyed to high-speed industrial output and working conditions. It was also conducted with an eye to what Lockheed referred to as 'recent industrial unrest.' Those applicants revealing mechanical training and aptitude, an even temperament and average, not exceptional, intelligence were acceptable for training and employment.*

45. Rondal Partridge recalls that it was Dorothea Lange who made the initial contacts with WPA officials in San Francisco which resulted in his NYA commission to photograph California youth in the spring of 1940 (interview with Partridge at his home in Berkeley, California, May 13, 1986). On Partridge's informal photographic apprenticeship to Dorothea Lange, see Karin Becker Ohrn, *Dorothea Lange and the Documentary Tradition* (Baton Rouge, 1980), 56, 69, 99, 174, 211.

National Youth Administration photographers make a pictorial record of NYA projects, furnishing their own cameras which include such diverse types as the two shown here.

*87*

Audience leaving NYA
exhibit building after showing
of the new movie, "Youth on
the Industrial Front." Illinois
State Fair. August 1941.

88

Boys taking test on softball
rules. San Marcos, Texas.
June 30, 1939.

89

*Rondal Partridge*

Migrant youth in potato field. Kern County, California. This is a characteristic costume of women in the potato fields. This girl came from Oklahoma, but has lived in Kern County long enough to be considered a resident. April 9, 1940. [A caption for a related picture from same series adds these details: "This girl came from the OK state three years ago and lives with her father in a rural slum in Wasco, Kern County, where they have settled down; their jobs in peas, potatoes and cotton are obtained less by the hit-and-miss methods and more by knowing local contractors and independent farmers. They are now considered 'locals' in the community in which they live. The girl never had a chance to finish high school and will be nineteen 'come August 11.' While the girl and her father are away from Wasco on jobs, they live in the trailer in which they came from Oklahoma."]

*90*

*Barbara H. Wright*

Young mountaineers watch–
ing a WPA movie (out of
doors) "The River." Mis–
souri. [Ca. 1939.]

*91*

Rondal Partridge

On the freights. He said he quit high school after two years, hung around home for a couple of years, and then got work as general kitchen help in a hotel. He had just been fired from a job of this kind in Los Angeles where he had "blown up" and "told the cook off." He carried a clean white shirt and was prepared to look for work when his money was completely gone. "I don't know where I'll go. Huntin' for a job I guess. I didn't go home—I'm on the bum. These agency jobs; you gotta buy them and I ain't got the dough." He talked about going to Redding, to Eugene, and to Seattle. He had $1.80. Yuba County, California. April 13, 1940.

Taking tap dancing lesson
from supervisor. San Marcos,
Texas. June 30, 1939.

Arts and crafts. South Side
Boys Club. Chicago, Illinois.
March 1937.

*Barbara H. Wright*

Student suspending wooden
plane model in wind tunnel.
New York University, New
York, New York [Ca. 1940.]

95

Radio. An all night session of
the Rag Chewers Club. NYA
Quoddy [Maine] Photography
Workshop.

96

Radio. This is a television receiving set which the boys constructed themselves. Some of the boys who are in the advanced stage are quite familiar with the science of television. NYA Quoddy [Maine] Photography Workshop. [The photographer is identified only as Lutter.]

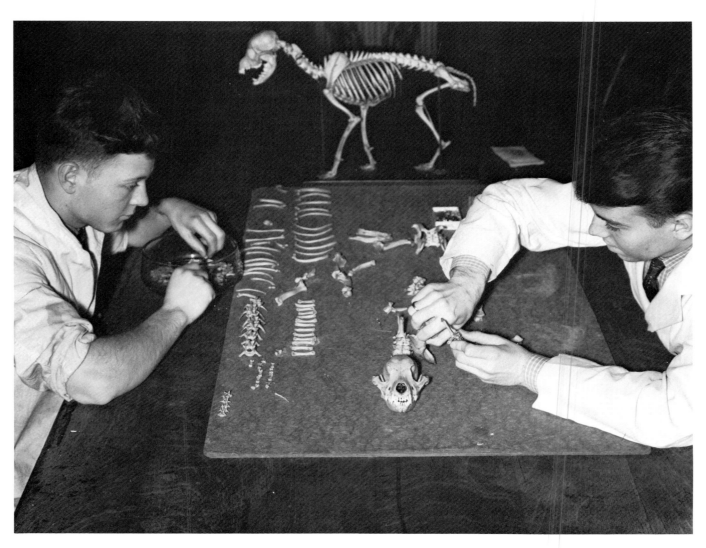

97

*Barbara H. Wright*

Student aid. George Washington University Biology Department. Boys' preparing skeletons for class exhibits saves University $35 to $50 per model.

San Francisco children wait-
ing for stockroom of Toy
Loan Library to open. San
Francisco, California.

N.Y.C. Naturalization Service, Immigration Bureau,
"Clerical." NYA assistance
has increased the clerical output of the Bureau of Immigration by 50 percent. Two
hundred seventy-five file
clerks, typists, stenographers,
and general clerical assistants
are learning their jobs in an
atmosphere of strict attention
to the serious implications of
their work. NYA workers
and the regular Civil Service
staff work side by side. New
York, New York.

100

NYA boys doing clerical
work for REA. Washington,
D.C.

*101*

NYA girls applying delicate
tints to pictures for use in
Buffalo [N.Y.] schools.

102

YWCA day nursery. NYA
youth teaches children how to
form clay figures. Washington, D.C.

NYA air mechanics unit.
South Charleston, West Virginia. [The photographer is probably Barbara H. Wright as related shots from the same site are credited to her.]

Josephine Rincon gets a lesson
in table setting from Mrs.
Hunter, instructor on the
NYA project in Los Angeles
County. All types of domestic work are included in the
courses given here to girls
who look forward to well-
paying jobs in this field.
Whittier, California.

105

*Dan Nichols*

Preparing free lunches by NYA girls for NYA youth on defense work. Filling containers with hot beef soup. Sample lunch consists of beef soup, sandwich, apple sauce, and a piece of ginger bread. Washington, D.C. [One of many pictures with captions detailing lunch preparation since free lunch was a significant additional incentive given low wages on NYA programs.]

106

NYA workers at Missouri
State Fruit Experiment Station. [The photographer is
probably Barbara H. Wright,
who in 1939 photographed
other scenes—mostly boys
picking fruit in the orchard—
at the Missouri State Fruit
Experiment Station.]

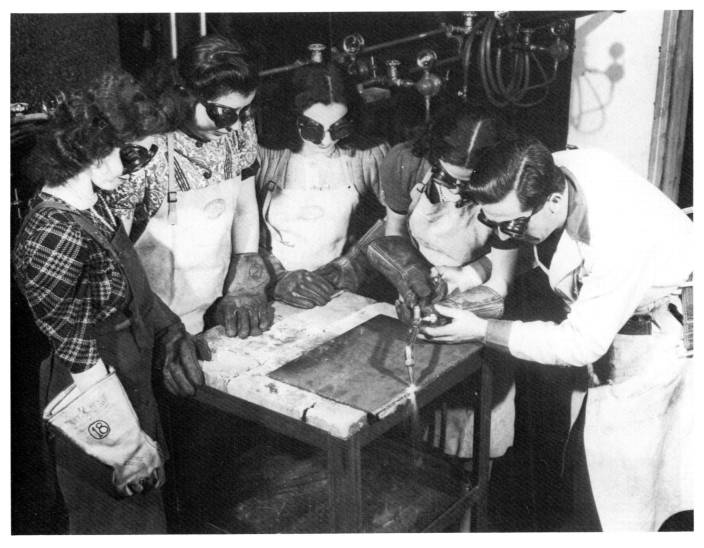

107

*Harold Corsini*

Girls at machine in the welding shop of the NYA Astoria Work Experience Center. The young women are being assigned to the mechanical and metal trades workshops to give them experience in defense activities. The center, the largest of its kind in the country, employs more than three thousand young men and women in its automobile repair, sheet metal, furniture, upholstery, welding, sewing, and painting shops. Queens, New York. December 20, 1940. New York NYA Photographic Workshop.

108

NYA participants in mobilization parade. New York
NYA Photographic Work-
shop.

*109*

*Barbara H. Wright*

Machine shop of NYA Huron
Work Experience Center. NYA
girls working on metal lathes,
part of an order for the Rock
Island Arsenal. Chicago,
Illinois.

Betty Maron poses in welder's "jeep" . . . [a] functional garment created by design department of NYA for women defense workers. [The] "jeep" is one piece, of blue and white striped denim. Long sleeves protect from flying sparks and spattering metal. Fitted wrists and ankles permit wear of safety gloves and shoes. Chicago, Illinois. [Based on the caption to a related "fashion shot," the photograph was made in August 1941.]

Ann Sheehan models pinafore uniform originated by design department of NYA for Illinois, consisting of white piqué pinafore apron over green and white cotton print. Designed for wear by NYA cafeteria workers, the outfit is smart enough for general home use. Chicago, Illinois. August 1941.

Colored division of NYA of
Georgia.

NYA Huron Work Experi-
ence Center. Scene in
machine shop, repairing parts
for other machines for Arsenal. Left to right: Mrs. Ora
Stokes; Mrs. Mary McLeod
Bethune; Michael J. Howlett;
Leonard Cooper, youth
worker, and Leo Kochin,
youth worker (both working
on engine lathe); and Mr.
Wendell, Supervisor in the
Machine Shop. Chicago,
Illinois.

*114*

Auto mechanics shop. Repairing the engine of a government official car. Charleston, West Virginia. [The photographer may have been Barbara H. Wright, as a large number of the West Virginia industrial shots are identified as her work.]

115

Food Service. Chicago,
Illinois. [The site is probably
the NYA Huron Work Expe-
rience Center which was
extensively photographed.]

*116*

NYA boys outside work
training center. Detroit,
Michigan.

*117*

NYA girls in welding
training program outside
workshop. Detroit, Michigan.

# WOMEN MAKE TOOLS OF WAR

HANDS that used to rock the cradle today run the lathe and the punch press. Five hundred thousand women hold responsible jobs in war industry, and by the end of the year more than 2,000,000 will be working in factories.

In aircraft and ammunition plants, in radio and machine shops, women work on wings and fuselages; assemble, load and inspect tracer bullets and fuses, and do hundreds of other jobs. Most women in war work had little previous industrial experience. Many were trained at defense schools and National Youth Administration work centers.

NYA-trained is 18-year-old Reba Connert, a shaper operator at a Peoria, Illinois, wire plant. Her graduation from a clerical job to an industrial career is told in pictures on this page.

["Women Make Tools of War," *Parade,* March 29, 1942, 13. Courtesy *Parade.* Uncredited photographs by Ann Rosener for Illinois NYA.]

**ALTHOUGH SHE HAD NO TRAINING,** Reba Connert decided last year she would do defense work.

**SO SHE SAID GOODBYE** to her job as a stenographer in a Peoria, Illinois, dry cleaning establishment.

**JOINING UP** with the National Youth Administration defense work center, she learned to recognize tools.

**AT THE NYA SCHOOL,** Reba received instruction in lathe operation, and in the use of milling machines.

**AFTER 100 HOURS** of machine shop training she was qualified to go and look for a real job in industry.

**SHE FOUND ONE** in a Peoria wire plant engaged in war work, and stepped into line to punch the clock.

**REBA'S JOB** at the wire works is running a shaper, which shapes the metal to the proper specifications.

**ON HER DAY OFF** Reba usually goes out with her boy friend, Corporal George Johnson, U. S. Army.

119

*Rondal Partridge*

At the time the University of California Peace Strike was held, the regular ROTC classes practiced marching—notice the posture, shoes. University of California, Berkeley. April 19, 1940. [In the caption to a related picture, the photographer noted that some members of ROTC had cut the drill to attend the strike rally.]

120

*Rondal Partridge*

Students listen to the speaker at the peace strike. University of California, Berkeley. April 19, 1940. [For the photographer's general caption to his series on the Berkeley Student Peace Strike, see note 43.]

121

*Rondal Partridge*

"Shipping day" in a Navy enlistment office. One of the solutions to getting tired of hanging around. A group of accepted Navy recruits receiving last instructions before they actually sign up for enrollment. Interviewed, all of them gave as their reason for enlistment the desire to learn a trade. Most of these boys come from rural areas; one third of them had discharge papers from the CCC. San Francisco, California. May 9, 1940. [The photographer noted in a related caption: "Enlistment is for six years; it was raised from four years July 1, 1939."]

*122*

*Rondal Partridge*

Roadside repair. On their way to the hill climb, this motorcycle party stopped by the roadside while one of their machines was repaired. The girls were pillion seat riders. Santa Clara County, California. April 5, 1940.

123

*Rondal Partridge*

Swing enthusiasts crowding
against the local bandstand at
an appearance of the Benny
Goodman band in a local
dance hall. One of the boys in
the foreground has a copy of
*Hot Jazz* by Hughes Panassie.
Oakland, California. April 26,
1940.

124

*Rondal Partridge*

Making out preliminary applications in the waiting line to the Lockheed employment office. Los Angeles, California. April 29, 1940. [See note 44 for the general caption to Partridge's series on job applicants at Lockheed.]

125

*Rondal Partridge*

Hanging around. Waiting for the movie house to open at 1 P.M. Sunday in the small San Joaquin Valley town of Tu-lare. The boy is an enrollee of the CCC. Madera County, California. May 1, 1940.

*Rondal Partridge*

Youth on relief. Young agricultural migrant buying a secondhand hat and shoes in the Oakland Salvation Army store. NYA has found that shoes are one of the most important needs of underprivileged youth and one of the first things they buy with NYA money. Oakland, California. April 18, 1940.

127

*Rondal Partridge*

Lockheed Testing Program. One brief newspaper article and youth of all ranges of mechanical ability, temperament, and intelligence crowd the State Employment Service. Oakland, California. April 23, 1940. [The photographer's caption to another picture from the series explains that the applicants in line are waiting for a routine interview before being tested for intelligence and temperament by Lockheed's personnel manager; see note 44 for Partridge's general caption outlining the objectives of the testing program.]

Job hunting. New York,
New York. May 7, 1940.
[The photographer is identified only as Nukanen; the file
photograph bears the stamp
of the New York NYA Pho-
tographic Workshop.]

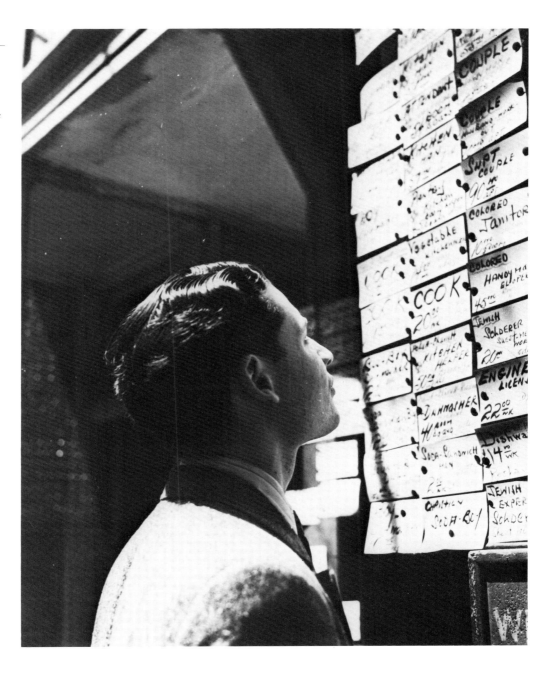

*129*

NYA girls in project dark-
room. [The back of the
photograph bears the stamp,
"Made by NYA Resident
Project, Camp Roosevelt,
Ocala, Florida."]

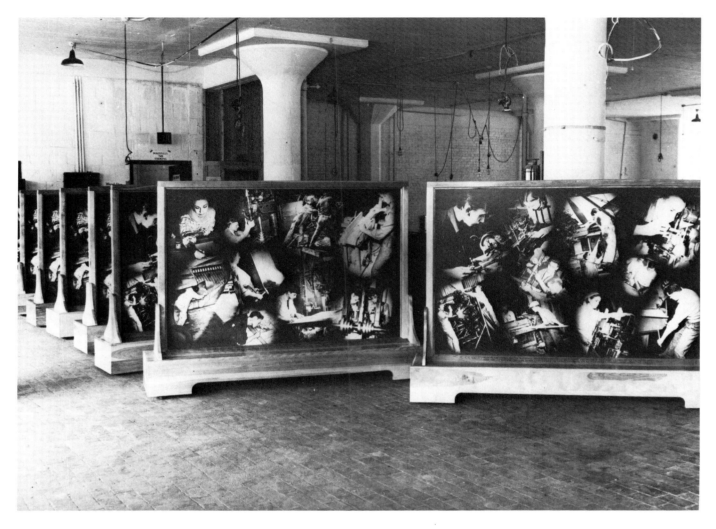

NYA exhibit building, Illinois State Fair. Springfield, Illinois. August 1941.

# Art and Document:

*Photography of the Works Progress Administration's Federal Art Project*

## Merry A. Foresta

Given the economic situation in the early 1930s in America, there was some question whether art could survive. Much of the patronage on which artists had traditionally depended had disappeared, and many artists, photographers among them, were hard pressed simply to maintain themselves. Late in 1933, after considerable artistic and political debate, an unprecedented program called the Public Works of Art Project (PWAP) was launched by the government, paid for out of relief funds. The Roosevelt administration's initial foray into art patronage was successful but short-lived. During the winter of 1933–34, the PWAP employed artists, including painters, sculptors, and printmakers, who were in need of work and had professional credentials. The PWAP was part of the first national work-relief effort, the Civil Works Administration, but because work-relief was extremely controversial and accepted only as a stopgap measure, funding was ended in the spring of 1934. Support for new, more permanent programs increased as it became clear that the Depression represented a long-term crisis and that short-term emergency measures were not enough.

The New Deal set up a number of more ambitious projects, with different administrators, goals, and constituencies, but which functioned together to give comprehensive support and encouragement to art and artists. The largest and most famous of these, the Works Progress (later Work Projects) Administration's Federal Art Project (WPA/FAP) which was active from 1935 through 1943, sought to aid artists by employing those who were already on relief. It focused on large cities, where most artists lived, and the work produced was available to state and municipal, rather than federal, institutions. The WPA/FAP employed as many artists and artisans and served as much of the public as funds permitted.[1]

To the artists the projects constituted a remarkable advance. "For the first time in our history the government supports art, assigns tasks to painters, sculptors, graphic artists and teachers, or accepts their freely created work, and pays a weekly wage," Meyer Schapiro observed in the November 1936 issue of *Art Front*. "The projects may be limited and the conditions poor, but the whole program is an immense step toward a public art and the security of the artist's profession."[2] In the 1930s artists embraced their role in society—for many it was the first time they felt they had any role to play. Beyond direct financial benefit, the social, psychological, and professional effects of the WPA/FAP programs were potent encouragement. In turn, administrators of the art programs sought to establish a community of artists that would nurture the cultural life of the country. In anticipation of a new era that never fully dawned, many artists naively rejoiced in the New Deal notion that art might come to be considered a public resource and that the ultimate patron might be the public. Others, however, including the public itself, did not agree as wholeheartedly. Like its predecessor, the PWAP, the WPA/FAP found itself under attack from critics who disapproved of a federally supported art program.

In 1936 a heavily illustrated national report, produced by the Washington office, stressed the importance and quality of art projects to counter the charges of "boondoggling" that Congress and the conservative press had leveled at the WPA/FAP since its inception. Holger Cahill, national director of the FAP, argued that the report was created "not only to document our accomplishment, but to do this in a unique and persuasive manner."[3] It included statements by artists, and highlighting their prose were convincing photographs by WPA/FAP photographers showing the variety of works of art produced by painters, sculptors, and printmakers. Photographs dramatized the activity of community art centers and emphasized teaching workshops. Indeed, the national report was, in Cahill's words, "a vivid summary in words and pictures."[4]

Primarily, photography was used as a tool of the FAP Department of Information. Among the achievements listed by the WPA/FAP in September 1938 were 355,126 photographs. For the most part these photographs were made for the record, and consisted of straightforward shots of project works of art and activities. Photography as an art, as opposed to a mere craft, was practiced significantly only in New York and California. In New York especially, the FAP encouraged photographers to attempt expressive projects, and many like David Robbins produced images evocative of the era's emotional climate (fig. 131). Of all the government-sponsored art programs the WPA/FAP—divided into the areas of Fine Arts, Practical Arts, and Art Education—employed the widest range of artists. Fine Arts divisions were designated easel, graphic, mural, and sculpture, and employed about half of the FAP personnel. The division of Practical Arts included the Index of American Design, and poster, craft, diorama, and photography projects. Art Education involved teaching art, the establishment and administering of community art centers, and research.

In addition to providing illustrations for the 1936 national report that quelled the immediate criticism of the project, photographs pictured all aspects of these government-sponsored art activities. Photographers documented FAP art exhibitions, and sometimes these photographs of art works were themselves turned into educational exhibitions, such as the "Frontiers of American Art" show that toured nationally in the late 1930s. An exhibition of photographs made at various FAP art education centers throughout the country also toured to other art centers. Photographs demonstrated the effectiveness of the projects by showing artists at work; photographers assessed the program at the same time as they were employed by it. For example, New York FAP photographer Eliot Elisofon worked with New York FAP sculptor Chaim Gross to document the steps involved in making a wood carving. The results provided an excellent advertisement for a successful and active program. The National Archives list of FAP photographs includes pictures of children's art classes and classes in ceramics, printmaking, sewing, or the making of ship figureheads. Photographs documenting the installation and dedication of major works of art, such as murals, often appeared in the style sections of newspapers. Contemporary journals such as *Art Front* frequently used FAP photographs to illustrate articles and book reviews.

Projects for photographers were not limited to the fine art sections of the program. Along with researchers and draughtsmen, photographers worked on the Index of American Design to create a comprehensive archive that would serve as a reference for designers, manufacturers, and historians (fig. 132). Many photographers provided illustrations for the Federal Writers' Project. New York photographer Max Yavno worked on the Federal Theater Project and the Federal Dance Project where he photographed backdrops, designed backdrops from photographs, and made glamorous publicity portraits of the actors (figs. 133, 134). In another division photographers were an integral part of the Timberline Lodge Project, sponsored as a Special Project by the FAP. As this Oregon recreation lodge was designed, built, and furnished by local artisans, photographers carefully documented the process, leaving a meticulous record of this model project (fig. 135).

Before the Depression the majority of FAP photographers had been commercial photographers or photojournalists, and while they considered themselves skilled craftspeople, few defined themselves as artists. Nonetheless, many of the images that remain from these photographers in the holdings of the National Archives are artfully made. A photograph of a young girl in a children's art class by Sol Horn is typical of many of the photographs made to document WPA activities (fig. 136). Skillfully lit, the photograph emphasizes both the pretty profile of the girl and her arm as it draws. Horn's photograph subtly connects the real girl and the one she is drawing, suggesting that art does indeed have an important connection to life.

A wider appreciation for art and the dissemination of visual information to the public were important aspects of the FAP. While artists—painters, sculptors, printmakers, craftspeople, filmmakers, and photographers—took delight in the freedom and opportunity the program afforded, Cahill had a serious philosophical purpose in mind as he formulated his FAP programs. From the beginning, Cahill and his associates attempted to define the role of art and the artist in society. If for the first time the government officially acknowledged the profession of being an artist, in return a serious social obligation was, if never required, implied. Cahill challenged each artist to attempt to define the scope of and the relationship between his or her social and creative activities.

Originally Cahill was impressed by the philosophy of John Dewey, whose pragmatic interpretation of human activity, as a program developed to solve individual and social problems, had inspired and entertained both scholarly and lay audiences earlier in the century.[5] Cahill understood Dewey to define art as "a mode of interaction between man and his environment."[6] So inspired, Cahill attempted to translate his own ideas about the social role of art into a program of action. For Cahill, the richest resources available to the artist were those aspects of the environment created by human society. Of special interest was "the stored up environment of the past, the tradition of art which is the result of prolonged and cumulative interaction between man as artist and his environment."[7] In Cahill's view, formal qualities in art were subordinate to the subject of human activity. The significant role that fine and practical art could play as a means of social communication and change was the strongest counter to criticism of government support of artists in America. Photographers, craftspeople, and artisans were allowed on the FAP relief "by virtue of skills and knowledge."[8] Cahill asked only that projects not classed as "fine arts" be "socially useful," and many photographers understood the work that they produced in terms of a larger social commitment. New York FAP photographer Arnold Eagle notes that there "always was a feeling of service, a desire to give back something for the relief that had been offered."[9]

Beyond the documentation of WPA/FAP art programs and finished works of art, the FAP photographers took on a wide range of special projects that emphasized work by the artist-photographers. According to Ralph Gutieri, a photographer and one of the directors of the Photography Division, the WPA "made no effort to predetermine the material which the individual photographers chose. Rather the choice of subject lay with the photographer on the basis of a system known as the 'creative assignment.' "[10] While never given the status of the painters on the FAP easel projects, photographers who had a creative project approved worked independently and had no need to report for daily assignments. The freedom to select and edit projects also distinguished FAP photographers from other government photographers, such as those hired by the Farm Security Administration (FSA). While the FSA photographers—for the most part from urban centers—traveled through areas unfamiliar to them, such as the rural South, concentrating on pictures requested by a central office in Washington, FAP photographers worked over a longer period of time closer to home.

Arnold Eagle was already interested in documenting social situations throughout New York City when he began to work on "creative" projects for the WPA. Though not a member, Eagle, by his own account, worked in the tradition of the New York Photo League. Organized in 1936 by still photographers who had broken away from the Film and Photo League, the New York Photo League influenced an entire generation of photographers. Known as "The League," it defined photography as a social document, insisting that photographers had an obligation to preserve and record the world in which they lived. Attention to the social environment and awareness of political and economic struggles were all necessary to the photographer's art. Just as earlier the Film and Photo League, founded in 1930 as a cultural wing of the Workers' International Relief, had used photographs to illustrate the lives and struggles of the American worker in publications such as *New Masses* and *Daily Worker,* Photo League members also used photography as an instrument for information and education. At the Photo League, however, documentary photography also had potential as an art form. The League offered lectures and classes, provided darkrooms, produced photographic projects (on areas such as Harlem and the

Chelsea district of New York City), and published *Photo Notes,* an irregular monthly bulletin. With a documentary style that effectively balanced the subject of a picture with aesthetic considerations, photography could, they believed, reveal unjust social conditions or alert the public to the richness of a community.

Like his colleagues at the League, Eagle was committed to a style of photography that was "believable, not artificial, convincing because it had a message." His series of photographs about a Hassidic Jewish community in Brooklyn was already underway in 1936 when Eagle began to work as a FAP photographer (figs. 137, 138). The project to "document a changing way of life and capture a shrinking community before it disappeared" was completed as a creative project under the auspices of the government.[11]

Eagle, with David Robbins, produced one of the most important photography assignments of the New York FAP. Knowing of the efforts by the Citizen Housing Council to find or build adequate shelter for the poor, in 1937 the two photographers began photographing the slums, where, in Franklin Roosevelt's words, "one third of a nation" was now forced to live.[12] Together and separately Eagle and Robbins spent months in the East Side and Chelsea districts of New York City in search of images for their series (figs. 139–142). Photographs of street life were balanced by interior portraits. All the pictures reveal both the horrible living conditions of the slums and the dignity of the people who live in them. Grouped in a series titled "One Third of a Nation," Eagle's and Robbins' work joined another three hundred photographs from service and creative assignments—including photographs for the Federal Writers' Project Guide Books, motion picture stills, photo murals, and experimental color photographs—in "East Side–West Side," a 1937 exhibition at the Federal Art Gallery on New York's prestigious 57th Street (fig. 143). There they received critical and political attention from none other than First Lady Eleanor Roosevelt.

While the "East Side–West Side" title related the exhibition to such issues as slum clearance, crime prevention, and education for public health, the photographs also demonstrated the artistic and technical side of the division's activities and its cooperation with civic agencies. According to Ralph Gutieri, who wrote the foreword to the exhibition catalogue,

*In any legislative program for better housing the photographic material included in this exhibition should play an important part. [It] portray[s] with full documentary evidence the need for further progress. As productions of the Federal Art Project they take a normal place in recording the episodes of our amazing epoch.*[13]

While thousands of people enjoyed the photographs during the months they were on view in the gallery, photographs by Eagle and Robbins were also used as evidence for a Citizen Housing Council petition to Congress.

One of the best known and most successful of the creative projects was Berenice Abbott's "Changing New York." As she recalls, the original plan for this photographic enterprise was "to preserve for the future an accurate and faithful chronicle in photographs of the changing aspect of the world's greatest metropolis" (figs. 144, 145).[14] Abbott began the project on her return from Paris in 1929 but did not find official approval until 1935 when the FAP agreed to sponsor her documentation of New York. The government put Abbott on a salary of $35 a week and provided an assistant and a driver. Exhibited under the auspices of the FAP in several galleries and museums—most notably, in "New Horizons in American Art" at New York's Museum of Modern Art in 1936, and at The Museum of the City of New York in 1938—the images were also published in several magazines, including *House and Garden* and *Town and Country,* and in a variety of publications sponsored by social and religious organizations, such as *The Christian Science Monitor.* The book *Changing New York,* with an introduction and brief captions by Elizabeth McCausland, was published in 1939.

Abbott's project was among the most ambitious ever undertaken by a single photographer: a comprehensive study of New York, encompassing the city's architecture, activities, inhabitants, and above all, its transformation to a technological citadel. *Changing New York* was a product of her fascination with what she described as "the present jostling the past."[15] With diligence she pursued contrasts—old and new, grand scale and small, horizontal and vertical, deep shadow and direct light, congestion and desolation, monumentality and triviality. Her work also required her to be a thorough historian. First alone and then with research assistants provided by the FAP, she studied neighborhoods and architecture. To carry out her documentation she employed angle shots, bird's eye views, worm's eye views, and rooftop views.

She was thus able to discern the larger design of the city in the chaos of its details, establishing a superb tension between the modern confidence in technology and the necessity to hold onto the more fragile and human-scale dimensions of the past.

Abbott's "Washington Street No. 37, Manhattan" (fig. 146) shows us building piled against building, with towering skyscrapers—the tops of which we can't even see, seemingly too tall to be included in the picture—hovering over a smaller building whose residential status is confirmed by the laundry which hangs in a tattered profusion off the fire-escapes. Though we are beguiled by the skillful ability of the photographer to render texture and space through light and shadow, Abbott's contrast of the eccentricity of the diminutive home and the towering anonymity of the office building, the former threatened by the latter, suggests a human as well as architectural situation. The upheaval of building and people is told by the photographer's vantage point—the view from the vacant lot in which she stands to make the picture is only possible, we suspect, because of the demolition of other buildings that once had laundry hanging out the back.

Another Abbott photograph from the same series compares the skyscraper, representing the new god of technology, with the older architecture of a more tradiional church. "Rockefeller Center, Church of St. Nicholas in Foreground" (fig. 147) suggests some of the choices of modern society, the possible sacrifice of the old to the new.

Inherent in the culture of the 1930s was a tendency to retrospection, as if a balm for the era's difficulties could be found in the solutions to problems of an earlier period. Historical narratives and portraits of historical figures are a common subject in all the art forms during the 1930s. Especially in murals, painters such as John Stewart Curry, Jared French, and Clifford Beal spotlighted the human interest angle of American history, retelling regional stories of the Revolutionary or Civil War events. Abbott's pursuit and documentation of a vanishing world is no less a manifestation of this impulse. Just as Eugene Atget had labored to capture the undistinguished as well as noble aspects of turn-of-the-century Paris, Abbott sought to provide a chronicle that would reverberate with both the present and the past.[16]

Other photographers also attempted comprehensive series. Under the auspices of the FAP, Louisiana photographer Clarence John Laughlin began a documentation of southern Victorian architecture and culture, a project that would occupy him for the rest of his life. Some of his earliest FAP photographs, such as "The Old and The New" (fig. 148), picture pedestrian Victorian buildings rather than more stereotypical antebellum mansions. Reminiscent of storefront images by FSA photographer Walker Evans, Laughlin's work tries to capture the details evocative of change. The jumbled graphic advertisements of modern products almost obliterate the humble facade of a turn-of-the-century New Orleans corner café; they stand in sharp contrast to the empty second story, separated from below by an iron balustrade, with its long French door windows that speak of earlier, more leisurely times, now closed.

Certain projects presented more systematic studies. While working on the Florida project, Florence Randall prepared a portfolio of photographs of Seminole Indians that was not only artistically successful, but also ethnologically valuable (fig. 149). Minor White's creative project for the WPA Oregon Art Project in the late 1930s was to record iron-front buildings and historic mansions of early Portland before they disappeared in the wake of redevelopment. White's proposal was candid in its mix of curiosity and sentimentality: "To document by nostalgia, to try to evoke the sense of pride Portlanders sixty years ago must have felt in their new city."[17] A second series of photographs on the Portland waterfront was completed in 1939. Both series circulated as exhibitions under the auspices of the WPA while White continued working for the FAP as a teacher of photography and then as director of the La Grande Art Center, a small WPA center in eastern Oregon. By White's own admission the Portland series were based on Abbott's "Changing New York," and photographs such as "The Kamm Building" (fig. 150) share with Abbott's a sense of dramatic contrast and a profound feeling for materials, surfaces, and textures. Without doubt, these photographs provided the firm basis for White's career as an artist.

In the same retrospective spirit that liked to compare the present to an earlier, more distinguished history, Alexander Alland, supervisor for the photo mural division of the FAP in New York, created "Old and New Newark." Commissioned in honor of Newark's one-hundredth anniversary, the mural had three panels illustrating the city past and present. Overall the work presented a montage of views of 1836 Newark, made up of historical photographs and engravings of the river, buildings, storefronts, and vistas of Newark, carefully cropped of any contemporary reference (fig. 151). These were combined with similar views of "New" 1936 Newark. Originally created as collaged maquettes, the three parts were photographically enlarged and assembled as a mural for the Newark Public Library.

Alland saw this mural and others accomplished during this time (see fig. 152) as contributions to a broad cultural life, with influence beyond that of more traditional art. In a recent interview, Alland stressed the distinct advantages photography offered over painting as a mural medium. Once technology had made large-scale enlargement possible, a photographer could make a mural faster than a painter, and the realism of the photographic image might communicate the mural's message more effectively. Furthermore, the technology of photography was compatible with the new public role of architecture, one which efficiently served the public at work or leisure. The new streamlined building made possible through the combination of technology and design looked to photography for its public art. Ironically, this sense of expediency also suggested that photography was suitable because it, like the new architecture the photography murals adorned, was not going to last, but would be replaced by ever more modern designs.[18] Already in his 1932 catalogue introduction for the Museum of Modern Art exhibition "Murals by American Painters and Photographers," Julien Levy pointed out the special affinity of the new photography and the new architecture: "The photographer is particularly well equipped to meet the problems of mural decoration as posed by the modern architect and builder. . . . The new medium satisfies at once three primary requisites of modern building: speed, economy, and flexibility."[19]

Indeed the mural division placed a strong emphasis on experimentation, and photographers often incorporated techniques such as montage, double printing, negative printing, or advertising design. On the mural projects there was a clear interaction between photographers and painters. Thus there was little reason for Byron Browne, an established painter, to hesitate when asked to create the photographic mural "Recreation and Sports" (fig. 153) for the day room of New York's

Chronic Disease Hospital. The influence of techniques introduced by recently emigrated Bauhaus artists such as Moholy-Nagy prompted experimentation by both painters and photographers. In Germany Bauhaus artists had also been concerned with the interrelationship of art and society, having planned the institute's coordinated programs of art and design around a community system. American painters, photographers, and artists who crossed the bounds of single mediums, such as Leo Lances, used the Bauhaus techniques of montage and the flexible style of commercial design to energize the subjects of murals (fig. 154).

One of the most ambitious projects was a series of airport murals intended for Floyd Bennett Field that were to incorporate photographs of airplanes and airports taken by Dmitri Kessel and Wyatt Davis, the brother of painter Stuart, with paintings designed by Arshile Gorky. For reasons that are unclear, the plans were changed and the design was assigned to Newark Airport. Not surprisingly, the Administration Building and Terminal at Newark Airport was considered the most modern of its kind when completed by the federal government's Civil Works Administration (the forerunner of the WPA). While the central idea on which the photo murals and mural paintings were based was the depiction of forms that had evolved from aerodynamic innovations, the early history of aviation—the "romantic period" according to a supervisor's report—was to be depicted by Gorky's painting.[20] The later history, beginning with the first attempts to build flying machines, was considered a more appropriate subject for the photo murals. The mechanics of flying, the instruments and characteristic forms of airplane construction, would best be represented by another form of modern technology—photography. Though the maquettes for the photo murals that Davis and Kessel created for the left wing of the building are preserved in the National Archives, the montage images of planes with details of instrument panels and blueprint drawings of engine sections were never installed (figs. 155 and 156). Ironically, a photographic record was made of every step of the installation of Gorky's mural. As the murals were later covered over, the photographs for years remained the only reference to these important paintings.

Only one FAP photography project was organized with the sole purpose of self-expression for the artists.

This FAP group, centered in southern California but with members as far north as San Francisco, was distinct from the other photographic groups in the state whose primary aim was photo-documentation of the art works and projects of the FAP. The photographers were Edward Weston, Brett Weston, Chandler Weston, Sonya Noskowiak, Sybil Anikeyev, Nacho Bravo, Hy Hirsh, William Abbenseth, and LeRoy Robbins. They produced shows of their work, which were distributed or given to museums, universities, schools, and public institutions. As part of an art bank that made works available to the public through institutions, individual prints were also distributed to offices, lobbies, and libraries. LeRoy Robbins recounts that it was "solo work" and that the photographers on the project "were lucky that somebody decided to include us in." As for the project's aesthetic concerns, he adds: "Probably, but incidentally, it helped elevate photography into the area of fine art."[21]

If the New York photographers were heirs to the Photo League tradition, the California photographers carried on the legacy of Group F-64. Active on the West Coast during the 1930s, the photographers in this informal organization produced unmanipulated, crisp images—in contrast to an earlier tradition of softly focused pictorialism. Several of the members, including F-64 founder Edward Weston, were among the FAP photographers. Edward's son Brett was supervisor of the project. Though clearly not as occupied with social themes as the East coast photographers, this western branch of the FAP did not completely abandon themselves to aesthetic concerns. The clean, straight look of their images implied a sense of truth and honesty in their pictures, and occasionally they chose subjects that subtly included references to the economic or social issues of the period. "Oranges" (fig. 157) by LeRoy Robbins, for instance, challenged the FSA photographer's version of rural hardship with a picture literally brimming with the results of a healthy harvest. The effect of New Deal programs on increased production is highlighted by the multitude of round oranges, their number and physical presence accentuated by the close-cropped frame of the image. Or, in another Robbins image, the lonely barrenness of a long Depression is suggested by the empty stretch of a seemingly endless highway (fig. 158). The poignant image "Music and Keys" (fig. 159) similarly implicates absence and loss. The title may refer to the possibility of

music making, but the lack of pianist implies the absence of human endeavor that could convert printed notes into the substance of music. The photograph becomes a metaphor of the era's lost dreams.

Known for elegant photogaphs with unusual grace of line and form, Edward Weston continued his work on the federal project, yet during this period of support he was also interested in making a photograph depicting modern power line structures. Though no demands were made on the photographers to choose relevant subjects, it is possible that Weston, now working for the government, self-consciously selected a scene that featured modern technology—the electric towers and the crucifix-like telephone poles—while also emphasizing the abstract pattern of the crossing wires.

For the most part, however, the old arguments about whether or not photography was art were remote questions during the New Deal. In a nation concerned with recovery from economic disaster, photographers, acting as visual historians, deliberately pictured the world around them for use by a variety of New Deal audiences. As record, instruction, and entertainment, photography aptly served the federal experiment in cultural enrichment for a larger audience. Beyond that, photography advanced upon the more traditional mediums, suggesting that it had an important role to play in the future of the nation's visual culture.

The most significant exhibition of photography sponsored by the FAP took place in 1937 at the Federal Art Gallery in New York. Entitled "Photography as Art and Document," it was the gallery's first show devoted solely to the work of the Photography Division of the project. Opening May 12, it was scheduled to close June 9, but by popular demand it remained on view throughout the summer and was visited and revisited by professional and amateur photographers and artists, as well as by the general public. Six photographers were represented by work produced on "creative assignment" and seven project cameramen exhibited work produced in the Photographic Division's service section. The exhibition included photographs by Arnold Eagle of old Hebrew scholars (figs. 137, 138) and devout old women performing traditional rituals; David Robbins' essay about the hard life of those who live and work along the waterfront of New York harbor (figs. 161, 162); several photo-montages by Cyril Mapass entitled "Theme and

Variation" (figs. 163, 164); and photographs of street vendors by George Herlick. Reviewers singled out Mark Nadir for his "lonely patterns from the bleak structures of the city" (fig. 165), and Andrew Herman for his documentation of the WPA Sewing Project with "some fine shots of workers hands" (fig. 166).

Art *and* document. As a tool for comunication, photography was used well and easily by the WPA/FAP. Though cast in a service role that had as its basis a sound realistic and recording function, photographers developed and perfected a documentary style that proved to be capable of more than simple reportage. Typical are the poignant yet descriptive scenes of food markets on New York City's Lower East Side by Andrew Herman (figs. 167, 168). To be documentary in a creative sense implies that the photographer has a point of view and an objective. For FAP photographers working on creative projects documentation meant an aesthetic: the imaginative and purposeful representation of the whole world seen by the camera eye—and by implication the human eye. On the occasion of photography's centenary, Abbott, then a FAP supervisor, commented on the significance of photography in 1937:

*Photographs of things and objects tell the story of mankind as much as the "candid" shot. In the past how have we learned about history? Not only from portraits and genre paintings, but also from the very rocks and stones, from the surviving architecture, from the things built by man. Photography has then a double range of communication, speaking to the present, but speaking also to the future and telling what sort of world it was.*[22]

Photography, one of the most versatile mediums supported by the WPA/FAP, was an art excellent at sensitive description (figs. 169, 170, 171). "In the bizarre happenings of everyday existence there is a fantastic unfamiliarity which the artist's conscious and deliberate effort could never duplicate, but which the camera eye will relentlessly capture," Berenice Abbott wrote in a 1937 review. She continued, "For this reason the photographic medium has caught the popular fancy as painting never has in modern times."[23] Using a style that suggested reality, photography could create the illusion of truth. As an information-bearing image, the photograph was readable, and for the most part the photographers working in the FAP—whether as reporters or as assemblers of creative projects—had a story to tell. The significance of photography during the 1930s was more and more evident: its use in magazines and books was the channel for reaching the average person. Without doubt, supported by the relief programs for artists, photographers were capable of images that educated, entertained, and inspired.

# Notes

1. The Treasury Department, which at that time built and administered federal buildings, also directed two art programs to provide decorations. One, the Treasury Relief Art Project (TRAP), functioned from 1935–39, and like the WPA/FAP, largely employed artists on relief. The other was the longest lived of these agencies, the Treasury Department's Section of Painting and Sculpture, later the Section of Fine Arts. For a full discussion of these federally supported art projects, consult Marlene Park and Gerald Markowitz, *New Deal for Art* (Hamilton, N.Y., 1977); Park and Markowitz, *Democratic Vistas: Post Offices and Public Art in the New Deal* (Philadelphia, 1984); and Richard D. McKinzie, *The New Deal for Artists* (Princeton, 1973).

2. *Art Front,* the journal of the Artist's Union, was published irregularly between November 1934 and December 1937.

3. Holger Cahill to Mrs. Ellen S. Woodward, assistant administrator, Women's and Professional Division, WPA, December 30, 1936, Cahill Papers, Archives of American Art. Quoted in Francis O'Connor, *Art for the Millions* (Greenwich, 1973), 30.

4. Quoted in O'Connor, *Art for the Millions,* 17.

5. See John Dewey, *Art as Experience* (New York, 1958; first published in 1934); and Bertram Morris, "Dewey's Aesthetics: The Tragic Encounter with Nature," *Journal of Aesthetics and Art Criticism* 30 (Winter 1971), 193.

6. Holger Cahill, "American Resources in Arts" (1939); first published in O'Connor, *Art for the Millions,* 34.

7. Quoted in O'Connor, *Art for the Millions,* 17.

8. McKinzie, *The New Deal for Artists,* 129.

9. Author's interview with Arnold Eagle, February 1986.

10. Ralph Gutieri, foreword to catalogue, "East Side–West Side" (New York Federal Art Gallery, 1938).

11. Eagle interview.

12. In his 1937 inaugural address Roosevelt declared, "I see one third of a nation ill-housed, ill-clad, and ill-nourished."

13. Gutieri, foreword to "East Side–West Side."

14. Berenice Abbott, "Changing New York," in Francis O'Connor, *Art for the Millions,* 158.

15. See note 14.

16. Abbott, who knew Atget in Paris during the 1920s, was responsible for rescuing his negatives from destruction at the time of his death. Abbott's relationship with Atget is well documented. See Berenice Abbott, *The World of Atget* (New York, 1964).

17. Minor White, *Mirrors, Messages, Manifestations, 1939–1968* (New York, 1969).

18. Author's interview with Alexander Alland, January 1986.

19. Julian Levy, "Photo Murals," in *Murals by American Painters and Photographers* (New York, 1932).

20. Ruth Bowman, *Murals without Walls: Arshile Gorky's Aviation Murals Rediscovered* (Newark, 1978), 24.

21. LeRoy Robbins correspondence to author, November 1985.

22. Berenice Abbott, "Photography, 1937–1939," *Art Front* (May 1937), 25.

23. See note 22.

131

*David Robbins*

[From the series *Along the Waterfront.*] New York City. 1937.

132

Mrs. Sterlling (artist finishes a
sketch of the Duncan Phyfe
table owned by Mrs. Griffith
for the Index of American
Design). Washington, D.C.
1936.

133

*Max Yavno*

Portrait of Therese Murray, Ingenue. Philadelphia, Pennsylvania. 1937.

134

*Max Yavno*

Dance Group. Philadelphia, Pennsylvania, 1939.

*135*

Exhibition of Timberline
Lodge Furnishings. Timberline, Oregon.

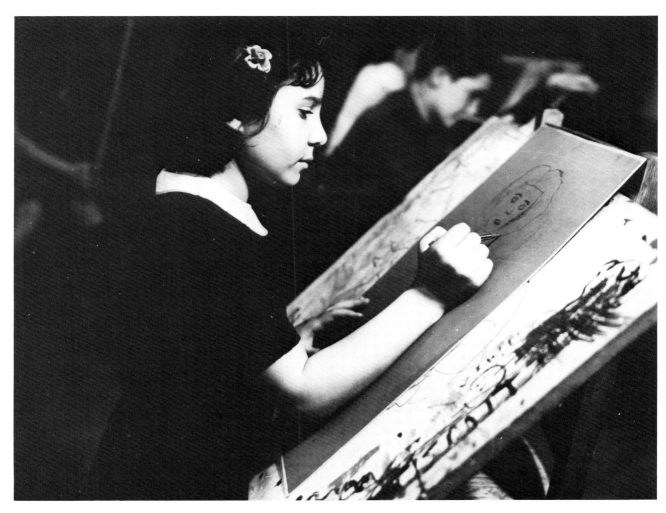

*Sol Horn*

Children's Art Class. New York City.

137

*Arnold Eagle*

The Talmud Student. New
York City East Side. 1935.

*Arnold Eagle*

Talmud Students. New York
City East Side. 1935.

139

*Arnold Eagle and*
*David Robbins*

[From the series *One Third of
a Nation*.] New York City.
1936–37.

*Arnold Eagle and
David Robbins*

[From the series *One Third of
a Nation*.] New York City.

*141*

*Arnold Eagle and*
*David Robbins*

[From the series *One Third of
a Nation.*] New York City.

142

*Arnold Eagle and
David Robbins*

[From the series *One Third of
a Nation*.] New York City.

[Review of "East Side–West Side" exhibition in Hebrew Language Newspaper. New York City. 1937. Photo copy courtesy of National Archives.]

*Berenice Abbott*

Brooklyn Bridge, Water and
Dock Streets [from the series
*Changing New York.*] New
York City. 1936.

145

*Berenice Abbott*

Greyhound Bus Terminal—
Manhattan [from the series
*Changing New York.*] New
York City. 1936.

*Berenice Abbott*

Washington Street No. 37,
Manhattan [from the series
*Changing New York*.] New
York City. 1936.

*Berenice Abbott*

Rockefeller Center, Church of
Saint Nicholas in Foreground
[from the series *Changing New
York*.] New York City. 1936.

*Clarence John Laughlin*

The Old and The New. New
Orleans, Louisiana. 1937.

*Florence Randall*

Seminole Indian. Florida.
[Circa 1937.]

*Minor White*

The Kamm Building. Port-
land, Oregon. 1938.

*Alexander Alland*

Old and New Newark. Photo
mural, Newark Public Li-
brary. Newark, New Jersey.
1938.

152

*Alexander Alland*

Approach to Manhattan.
[Sketch for photo mural.]
Riker's Island. New York
City. 1937.

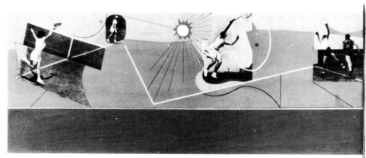

153

*Byron Browne*

Recreation and Sports. Photo
mural, dayroom of the
Chronic Disease Hospital.
New York City. 1940.

154

*Leo Lances*

Gymnastics. Photo mural,
WPA Community and Health
Building at the World's Fair.
New York City. 1939.

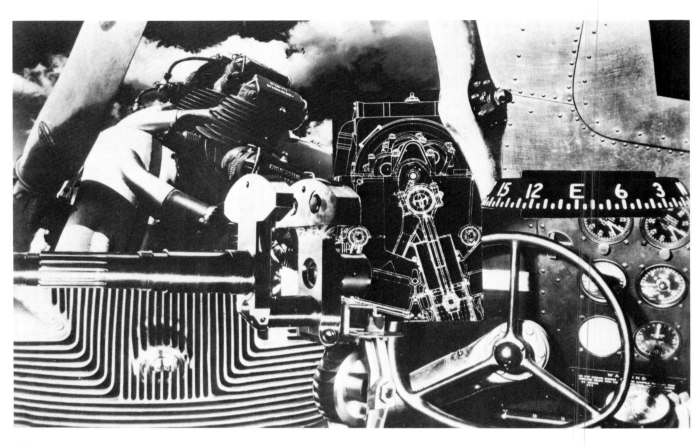

155

*Wyatt Davis*

[Detail of sketch for proposed
photo mural, Newark Air-
port.] Newark, New Jersey.
1936–37.

156

*Wyatt Davis and Dmitri Kessell*

[Proposed photo mural, Newark Airport.] Newark, New Jersey. 1936–37.

157

*LeRoy Robbins*

Oranges. California. 1936.

*158*

*LeRoy Robbins*

Highway. California. 1936.

159

*LeRoy Robbins*

Music and Keys. California.
1936.

*Edward Weston*

Power Lines, Lincoln Boulevard. California. 1936.

*David Robbins*

[From the series *Along the Waterfront*.] New York City. 1937.

*162*

*David Robbins*

[From the series *Along the Waterfront.*] New York City. 1937.

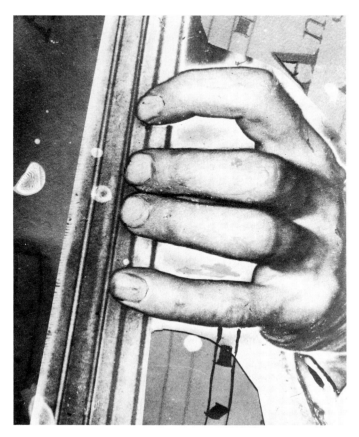

163

*Cyril Mypass*

[From the series *Theme and Variation*.] New York City. [Circa 1937.]

164

*Cyril Mypass*

Solarized Press. New York City. [Circa 1937.]

165

*Mark Nadir*

[Untitled creative assignment.] New York City. 1937.

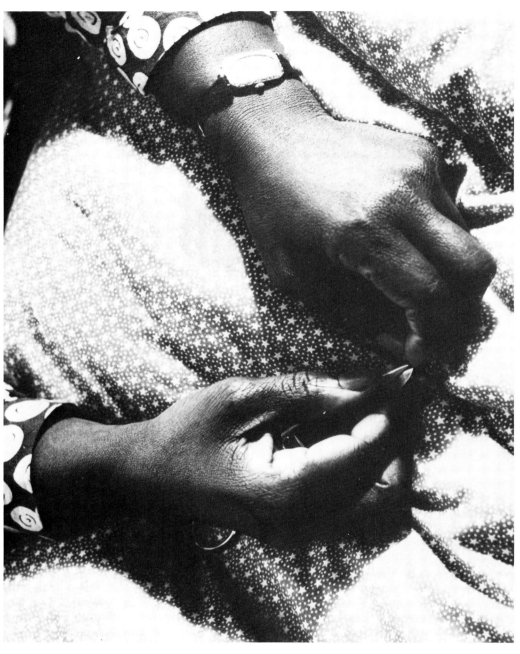

Andrew Herman

[Untitled assignment, Federal Sewing Project.] New York City. 1937.

Andrew Herman

[From the series *East Side Market Scenes*.] New York City. [Circa 1937.]

*Andrew Herman*

[From the series *East Side Market Scenes*.] New York City. [Circa 1937.]

Leo Lances

[From the series *Industry*.]
1937.

*Sol Libsohn*

[From the series *Food for New York City*.] 1939.

*Helen Levitt*

[Untitled creative assignment.] New York City. 1937.

# Photographic Sources and Credits

The documentary photographs reproduced in this book are primarily drawn from collections in the Prints and Photographs Division of the Library of Congress (LC) and the Still Pictures Branch of the National Archives (NA) and may be ordered by the following numbers. Prices and other information will be furnished on request from either repository. Documentation for illustrations not listed here is included in the captions.

## Farm Security Administration

Figure 1. USF 33 6135–M4 (LC)
Figure 2. USF 34 8114C (LC)
Figure 3. USF 33 6124.M5 (LC)
Figure 4. USF 34 9599 (LC)
Figure 7. USF Z62 11491 (LC)
Figure 9. USF 33 2927–M1 (LC)
Figure 10. USF 34 42268–D (LC)
Figure 11. USF 33 13008–M4 (LC)
Figure 12. USF 33 12980–M3 (LC)
Figure 13. USF 33 5183–M5 (LC)
Figure 14. USF 33 1720–M3 (LC)
Figure 15. USF 34 34057–D (LC)
Figure 16. USF 34 34020–D (LC)
Figure 17. USF 34 34028–D (LC)
Figure 18. USF 34 64240–D (LC)
Figure 19. USF 34 38251–D (LC)
Figure 20. USF 34 35281–D (LC)
Figure 21. USF 34 42905–D (LC)
Figure 22. USF 34 32501–D (LC)
Figure 23. USF 33 30523–M1 (LC)
Figure 24. USF 33 30209–M3 (LC)
Figure 25. USF 34 8587–D (LC)
Figure 26. USF 34 18774–D (LC)
Figure 27. USF 34 1780–C (LC)
Figure 28. USF 34 18545–D (LC)
Figure 29. USF 34 18616–C (LC)
Figure 30. USF 341 1829–B (LC)
Figure 31. USF 34 825 (LC)
Figure 32. USF Z62 50849 (LC)
Figure 33. USF 34 16223–E (LC)
Figure 34. USF 34 16129–C (LC)
Figure 35. USF 344 7744–2B (LC)

## United States Department of Agriculture

Figure 36. 33–S–16902c (NA)
Figure 37. 33–S–16828c (NA)
Figure 38. 33–FRA–S–18028c (NA)
Figure 39. 16–G–160–1–AAA–Ala.–61 (NA)
Figure 40. 145–AAA–5078w (NA)
Figure 41. 33–S–18152c (NA)
Figure 42. 33–S–4230 (NA)
Figure 43. 33–S–5164 (NA)
Figure 44. 33–S–5129 (NA)
Figure 45. 33–S–5310 (NA)
Figure 46. 33–S–20040c (NA)
Figure 47. 33–S–3589 (NA)
Figure 48. 16–G–112–2–S–3522A (NA)
Figure 49. 33–S–17876c (NA)
Figure 51. 16–G–167–3–8976A (NA)
Figure 52. 33–S–18668c (NA)
Figure 53. 33–FRA–S–18622c (NA)
Figure 55. 33–S–23891c (NA)
Figure 56. 16–N–59 (NA)
Figure 57. 16–N–1894 (NA)
Figure 58. 16–G–266–M&A–11509 (NA)
Figure 59. 16–N–1224 (NA)
Figure 60. 33–S–8584 (NA)
Figure 61. 16–G–52–2–17866 (NA)

## Civilian Conservation Corps

Figure 62. 35–G–830 (NA)
Figure 64. 35–G–4306–CN–3644 (NA)
Figure 65. SC–10,392 (USDA, Soil Conservation Service)
Figure 67. CN 3641 (NA)
Figure 68. CN 3640 (NA)
Figure 69. 35–G–2073 (NA)
Figure 70. 35–G–119 (NA)
Figure 71. 35–G–110 (NA)
Figure 72. 35–G–269–SCS–5 (NA)
Figure 73. 35–G–267 (NA)
Figure 74. 35–G–204 (NA)
Figure 75. 35–G–213 (NA)
Figure 76. 35–G–1067 (NA)
Figure 77. 35–G–31 (NA)
Figure 78. 35–G–818 (NA)
Figure 79. 35–G–540 (NA)

Figure 80. 35–G–441 (NA)
Figure 81. 35–G–34 (NA)
Figure 82. 35–G–26 (NA)
Figure 83. 35–G–568 (NA)
Figure 84. 35–G–440 (NA)

## National Youth Administration

Figure 86. 119–G–11E–1 (NA)
Figure 87. 119–S–11G–6 (NA)
Figure 88. 119–G–13–2 (NA)
Figure 89. 119–CAL–80 (NA)
Figure 90. 119–G–219–M (NA)
Figure 91. 119–CAL–13 (NA)
Figure 92. 119–G–13–1 (NA)
Figure 93. 119–G–2A–4046 (NA)
Figure 94. 119–G–109–D (NA)
Figure 95. 119–G–3250–D (NA)
Figure 96. 119–S–15C–1 (NA)
Figure 97. 119–G–12C (NA)
Figure 98. 119–S–2E–1 (NA)
Figure 99. 119–G–143–D (NA)
Figure 100. 119–G–19A–1 (NA)
Figure 101. 119–S–19U–2 (NA)
Figure 102. 119–G–850–D (NA)
Figure 103. 119–G–149–D (NA)
Figure 104. 119–S–5B–1 (NA)
Figure 105. 119–G–4109–D (NA)
Figure 106. 119–G–363–D (NA)
Figure 107. 119–S–20G–2 (NA)
Figure 108. 119–S–20D–3 (NA)
Figure 109. 119–3621–D (NA)
Figure 110. 119–S–12C–1 (NA)
Figure 111. 119–S–12C–2 (NA)
Figure 112. Lot LC 5344 (LC)
Figure 113. 119–S–16S–2 (NA)
Figure 114. 119–G–14–4208–D (NA)
Figure 115. 119–G–3446–D (NA)
Figure 116. 119–G–3408–D (NA)
Figure 117. 119–G–3627–D (NA)
Figure 119. 119–CAL–56 (NA)
Figure 120. 119–CAL–43 (NA)
Figure 121. 119–CAL–212 (NA)
Figure 122. 119–CAL–201 (NA)
Figure 123. 119–G–215 (NA)
Figure 124. 119–G–147 (NA)
Figure 125. 119–G–93 (NA)
Figure 126. 119–G–84 (NA)
Figure 127. 119–G–137 (NA)

Figure 128. 119–S–20D–8 (NA)
Figure 129. Lot LC 5344 (LC)
Figure 130. 119–S–11G–2 (NA)

## Works Progress Administration

Figure 131. 69–ANP–13–P759–70 (NA)
Figure 132. 69–AG–571 (NA)
Figure 133. 69–TC–PA–18–3 (NA)
Figure 134. 69–TC–PA–3–2 (NA)
Figure 135. 69–AG–1073 (NA)
Figure 136. 69–ANP–5–2888–9 (NA)
Figure 137. Courtesy of Arnold Eagle
Figure 138. Courtesy of Arnold Eagle
Figure 139. 69–ANP–1–P2329–48 (NA)
Figure 140. 69–ANP–1–P2329–24 (NA)
Figure 141. 69–ANP–1–P2329–84 (NA)
Figure 142. 69–ANP–1–P2329–6 (NA)
Figure 144. Courtesy of National Museum of American Art
Figure 145. Courtesy of National Museum of American Art
Figure 146. Courtesy of National Museum of American Art
Figure 147. Courtesy of National Museum of American Art
Figure 148. 69–AG–845 (NA)
Figure 149. 69–AG–1279–1 (NA)
Figure 150. Courtesy The Minor White Archive, The Art Museum, Princeton University. Copyright © 1982 Trustees of Princeton University.
Figure 151. 69–AN–10–P188 (NA)
Figure 152. 69–AN–10–P1603 (NA)
Figure 153. 69–AN–85–3966 (NA)
Figure 154. 69–AN–863–16 (NA)
Figure 155. 69–AG–395 (NA)
Figure 156. 69–AG–1125 (NA)
Figure 157. Courtesy of LeRoy Robbins
Figure 158. Courtesy of LeRoy Robbins
Figure 159. Courtesy of LeRoy Robbins
Figure 160. 69–AG–1281 (NA)
Figure 161. 69–ANP–13–759–31 (NA)
Figure 162. 69–ANP–13–759–133 (NA)
Figure 163. 69–ANP–9M–4 (NA)
Figure 164. 69–ANP–6–1722–5 (NA)
Figure 165. 69–ANP–11–724–12 (NA)
Figure 166. 69–ANP–4–702 (NA)
Figure 167. 69–ANP–3–P1732–6 (NA)
Figure 168. 69–ANP–3–P1732–35 (NA)
Figure 169. 69–ANP–6–1722–1 (NA)
Figure 170. 69–ANP–8–P3032–85 (NA)
Figure 171. 69–ANP–7–P3028–149 (NA)

# Contributors

Pete Daniel is curator of Agriculture and Natural Resources at the National Museum of American History, Smithsonian Institution. His most recent books are *Breaking the Land: The Transformation of Cotton, Tobacco, and Rice Cultures since 1880* and *Standing at the Crossroads: Southern Life in the Twentieth Century*. He has also written on documentary photography, specifically on the works of Frances Benjamin Johnston and on the use of documentary images during the 1927 Mississippi River flood.

Merry A. Foresta has been curator for Photography at the National Museum of American Art, Smithsonian Institution, since 1983. Prior to assuming that position, she was assistant curator in the Department of Twentieth-Century Painting and Sculpture. A graduate of Cornell University she also worked at the Herbert F. Johnson Museum of Art, Cornell University. She is the author of *Exposed and Developed Photography Sponsored by the National Endowment for the Arts*.

Maren Stange is assistant professor of Communications and American Studies at Clark University in Worcester, Massachusetts. Her book, *"Symbols of Ideal Life": Social Documentary Photography in America, 1890–1950*, is forthcoming in 1988. Winner of a Logan Award for New Writing on Photography and a contributor to *Prospects, Afterimage, Views,* and the *Boston Review,* she has held fellowships from the Center for Advanced Study in the Visual Arts, the American Council of Learned Societies, and the Smithsonian Institution.

Sally Stein is a cultural historian who has written extensively on the history of photography and on the modernization of print media. Her essays on the visual culture of the twenties and thirties include studies of photomontage, women's magazines, and the emergence of color photography. She has also produced a monographic essay on the FSA photographer Marion Post Wolcott. A former Smithsonian Fellow, she currently teaches in the Department of Visual Arts at the University of California, San Diego.